Richard Th
& Cathryn Wellner

CASTLES in the AIR

Music & Stories of
British Columbia's 1860s gold rush

A companion to
Rough but honest miner CD

Winter Quarters Press

Winter Quarters Press
Box 15 Miocene, Williams Lake, B.C., Canada V2G 2P3
(250) 296-4432; fax (250) 296-4429
e-mail: cwellner@grassrootsgroup.com
http://grassrootsgroup.com

Distributed by   Sandhill Book Marketing Ltd.
                  #99 - 1270 Ellis Street
                  Kelowna, B.C., Canada V1Y 1Z4
                  (250) 763-405; fax: (250) 763-4051

Canadian Cataloguing in Publication Data

    Wright, Richard Thomas, 1940-
        Castles in the air: music and stories of British Columbia's 1860s
    gold rush

    Each chapter gives historical background for the songs and narra-
        tions found on the CD Rough but honest miner.
    ISBN 0-9696887-5-X

        1. British Columbia—History—1849-1871. 2. British Colum-
        bia—Gold discoveries. 3. British Columbia—Gold dis-
        coveries—Songs and music—History and criticism. I.
        Wellner, Cathryn, 1946- II. Title. III. Title: Rough but
        honest miner.

    FC 3882.5.W75 2000   971.1'02   C00-900688-5
    F1089.C3W75 2000

Designed by Cathryn Wellner
Typesetting by Cathryn Wellner
The Typefaces are ITC Berkeley Oldstyle and Hobo
Printed and bound in Canada by Friesen Printers, Altona, Manitoba

Credits:
Photos: British Columbia Archives and Records Service (8, 10, 13, 14, 15, 17, 18, 19, 20, 21, 28, 30, 37, 42, 45, 49, 52, 64, 66, 68, 70, 76, 83, 89), Public Archives of Canada (cover, 29, 61, 75, 92), Toronto Metropolitan Library (57), Library of Congress (40, 27, 25, 77) Lester S. Levy Collection, Johns Hopkins University (17)
Except where noted, images used are in the public domain.
Map: Matthew Macfie, *Vancouver Island and British Columbia*, 1865

The Goldfields
of British Columbia

Edward Weller, *Vancouver Island and British Columbia,*
Mathew Macfie, 1865

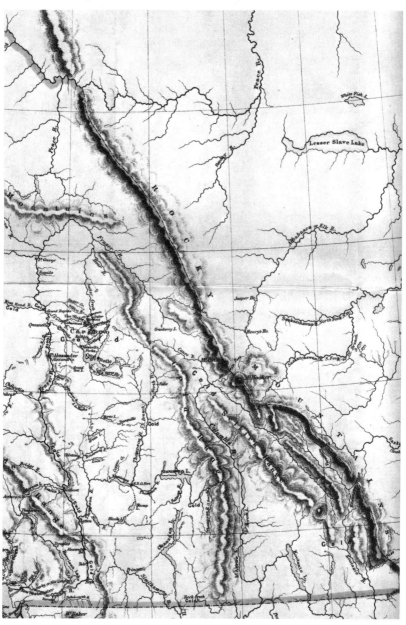

Acknowledgements

To our parents, for instilling in us a love for music.

To all those who have ever given us songs or music.

    The Boys from Joe Denny's for those early music years.

    Mike Ballantyne who helped us locate Johanna Maguire's song.

    The Mudcatters who helped find words and music at www.mudcat.org, in particular Bruce Olson and his great Web site, and Joe Offer.

    Benjamin Tubb for his collection of songs and midi files at www.pd.org and for preparing midi files for us for rehearsal and Bobby Horton for his great collection of Civil War CDs.

To all the Barkervillians we have worked with over the years.

To Phil Thomas, upon whose back anyone collecting songs in B.C. must ride.

A special thanks to Jennifer Iredale, curator with BC Heritage Branch, who encouraged, prodded and supported this project for years.

To the musicians and recording engineers who helped with this project and shared our enthusiasm.

    Ken Hamm, one of North America's premier blues musicians, was a great help in first encouraging us to go ahead and then in arranging studios, introducing us to musicians, advising on songs and arrangements, being our sounding board and generally supporting what turned into a big project.

    John and Michele Law, whom we knew from our sojourn in the Cowichan Valley and who are skilled, talented and popular musicians and songwriters, were a great help in getting the tunes down on tape, and in sharing their home with us for rehearsing.

    Donna Konsorado who not only plays a mean banjo but supplied us with cookies to die for.

Caridwen Irvine who brought the technical grounding of classical training to her fiddle playing.

Jerry Paquette, Raincoast Music wizard, whose studio gave us a sense of home, who jumped in to supply us with bass vocals, who mixes with the best and who kept the coffee flowing.

Jack Velker who turned the leaky bellows on a pump organ into a percussion instrument.

Bud Bremner of Coastal Mastering whose technical genius put the finishing touch on the CD.

Duncan Bell, whose deep voice and Scots accent gave us a new understanding and appreciation of James Anderson's poems.

Edd Wright, Richard's brother, whose remarkable voice is testament to his years in opera and musical theatre.

Len Osanic, Fiasco Bros., who knew how to draw out the best sound from the work of Edd, Duncan and Jack.

Willie P. Bennett, a real gentleman, who stepped in while on tour and helped us with several tracks.

Thanks to Sherry Edmunds-Flett who shared her research notes on the Gibbs family with us.

Our thanks to Jean Speare, a tireless workers for history and heritage, who recorded and edited the wonderful stories of Augusta Tappage and who gave us permission to use the Lillooet quote from her book *Days of Augusta*.

It is not possible to do historical research in B.C. without the collections of the B.C. Archives in Victoria, and without the assistance of the skilled and helpful staff it would be much more difficult. As always we owe a great vote of thanks to all the BCARS staff. Richard in particular owes a debt of gratitude for the help he received in filling out forms and requests while he laboured in the archives with a broken arm, unable to even scratch a note. Politicians and bureaucrats who would cut services and funding, for whatever reason, should either not read history or listen to this CD, or should loosen the purse strings and work to ensure not only the continuation but the expansion of this vital resource.

Thanks to all those who sell books and CDs, and to the Folk DJs of the world who continue to support the folk tradition.

And to all those who encouraged this project to move forward, in whatever way.

This book is dedicated to our parents, who taught us to love music
 Thomas Wright
 Edna Audrey Wright
 Joyce Holm

Cariboo Sentinel, July 29, 1871

Contents

Volunteer Rifle Corps Band outside Parliament Building, Victoria

Music as another way of viewing history

This project began as research into the songs and music that were sung and played in gold rush camps and towns in B.C. However, it soon became evident that what we really found was another way of viewing history, another way of understanding the life and times of a century and a half ago.

Until the Burrell letters were found by Jennifer Iredale, for instance, we could only guess at what music the hurdy fiddlers played.

Knowing the songs allows us to eavesdrop in a gold rush saloon, listen around an Overlanders' campfire and sit in the Theatre Royal with our ear tuned to 1860s music. We can hear the prejudices, the political voices, the hopes and dreams and laughter of the day when we listen to James Anderson or black miner J. Lawrence or Rebecca Gibbs. We can view the springtime rush to the creeks through the eyes of a Native woman.

Music has always given us another voice, allowing us to say things not normal in everyday speech. These songs reach into the past for an explanation of time. What is remarkable is that in many cases we sing the same songs today, six generations later.

In as many places as possible we have tried to include original documents or quotes that relate to the subject of the song so that you, the reader and listener, can make your own interpretation.

Richard has been collecting songs since he began writing down the words of songs sung around Scout campfires. He began collecting gold rush songs decades ago but became serious about it while working as a street interpreter or historical re-enactor and while singing with The Boys From Joe Denny's, a street band in Barkerville. Progress was slow, songs and music hard, if not impossible, to find.

It was not until the advent of the World Wide Web and the Internet that research of all kinds became more accessible. Libraries of sheet music suddenly were accessible from home, world-wide searches for music were possible and "mail lists" of esoteric subjects blossomed where researchers, scholars and musicians could exchange notes and thoughts.

Cathryn's interest in old music was nurtured by a singing family, summer youth camps, and Sunday mornings spent waiting for the sermon to end and the music begin. When she discovered, during a decade at the front of a classroom, that spinning a tale was a sure means of getting the attention of even the most recalcitrant student, she began gathering tales. Her distaste for history became fascination when she discovered the ordinary and colorful characters who had been left out of the textbooks.

The songs and poetry on this album cover a time period from the discovery of gold in 1858 until the decline of the goldfields' first boom in about the mid 1870s. Virtually all have been documented as having been sung, or written, in Barkerville, the Cariboo goldfields or Victoria.

All of them were popular during those couple of decades. The origin of some of the music is lost in the traditional-music past. Some tunes have been recycled again and again, each time telling a new story. The title is taken from James Ballantine's song *Rough but honest miner* and James Anderson's line, "There's miners more than one built this castle in the air."

Listen to these songs and imagine that it is 150 years ago. These were the hit songs of the day, sung around campfires, in parlours, in saloons. These are the tunes that men and women danced to, sang while they worked. These are songs that told their story. Listen and you will hear it.

Whoe'er may look
Into this book
And call this writing stuff—
It seems to me—
Whoe'er it be—
That Person is a Muff

'Tho not sublime,
At least, tis Rhyme—
But if you still deny it
And think you could
Make half as good
Why go to work, and try it—

J. Lawrence, Horsefly River, 1866

Bill Phinney, Caledonia Claim

The Rough
but Honest Miner

When the news of gold on the lower Fraser River leaked out and reached the coastal towns of Oregon and California, there was a rush like the world has never seen. The first two ships to leave California landed 1700 men at Fort Victoria on April 20, 1858. Over the summer some 30,000 men and women arrived, a massive migration into a British colony that had previously had a population of only about 600 Europeans, Hudson's Bay Company people and settlers.

The majority of these rushers were Americans from the goldfields of California, and many had experience gleaned from those creeks.

There were enough Americans that Governor Douglas worried about annexation by occupation, a refrain heard in the parody of Yankee Doodle which says, "Yankee Doodle wants a state, Oregon or Texas, Sends some squatters in it straight, And quietly annexes. Yankee Doodle, Doodle Do, Yankee Doodle Dandy, He can do the Britishers and Mexicans so handy."

The ditty referred to the way the U.S. had taken Oregon from the British by occupying the contested region. Annexation by occupation it was called. Annexationists in St. Paul, Minnesota, gave the Canadian government similar fears when they cast eyes on the Red River settlement around Fort Garry, later to be Winnipeg, Manitoba.

There were some tense moments on the lower Fraser that showed Douglas the need to bring in British troops. The Royal Engineers could provide not only engineering skills for the new colony but a military force to make sure the British Union Jack flew and not the Stars and Stripes.

James Anderson's song, *Rough but Honest Miner*, the album's title track, is set to the popular Scots song by James Ballantine, *Castles in the Air*, sung by many miners, overlanders and stage performers. Ballantine in turn had used the tune of *Bonny Jean of Aberdeen*. This tune was also used for *The Ball of Kirriemuir* and the Irish *The Stuttering Lovers*. It was printed at least 13 times in Scots song and tune books from 1725 to 1790.

Anderson, in an 1897 letter, considered this his best song/poem and said, "I would have been pleased had the other rhymes been buried in the tailings of Williams Creek. They were written on the spur of the moment, and for the moment, and are not worthy of reproduction."

Anderson, like many writers of the day, was not above borrowing a few phrases or lines, which he indicates with double quotes. The first four lines of the last verse are taken directly from *The Village Blacksmith*, the Henry Wadsworth Longfellow poem that was a popular song in the 1860s and 70s.

The lyrics here have been "translated" from Anderson's Scots dialect.

Anderson is able to take a few lines and explain the whole process of searching for gold and at the same time get into the mind of the miner. He was able to do this as he was first of all a miner and only wrote poetry and songs as an evening's pastime.

This was a popular song with Barkerville miners, even though Anderson is saying in his last verse that the only gold or stake miners are likely to see may well be in heaven, a true "castle in the air."

In this song Anderson has mixed Scots dialect with some Chinook words. In the last verse he says, "tho' his tum-tum may be sair." In Chinook tum-tum is not stomach but the "heart" or "will." Anderson is saying that even though the miner is heartbroken, even though his will may be sick or sore, he "has all the grit" and is continuing. He then adds that it is likely that the only strike or stake the miner will see is in heaven.

The Rough But Honest Miner

1.

The Rough but Honest miner
What toils night and day,
Seeking for the yellow gold
Hid among the clay—
Hawkin' on the mountain side,
What he does there
Ah! The old dreamer's
Building castles in the air.
His weather-beaten face
And his sore-worn hand
Are tell-tales to all
If the hardships that he stands;
His head may grow gray
And his face full o' care,
Hunting after gold
With its castles in the air.

2.

He sees the old channel
Buried in the hill
Filled full of nuggets—
So goes at it with a will,
For long weeks and months,
Driftin' late and early,
Cutting out a door
To his castle in the air.
He hammers at the rock,
Believin' it's a rim,
When ten to one 'tis nothing
But his fancy's whim—
Sure when he gets thro'
He'll find his hame-stake there;
There's miners more than one
Built this castle in the air.

3.

He thinks his pile is made,
And he's goin' home in fall—
He joins his dear old mother,
His father, friends and all,
His heart e'en jumps wi' joy,
At the thoughts of bein' there,
There's many a happy minute
Buildin' castles in the air.
But hopes that promised high
In the springtime of the year,
Like leaves of autumn fall
When the frost of winter's near
So his buildin' tumbles down
With another blast o' care
'Til there's no stone left standing,
Of his castle in the air.

4.

"Toiling and sorrowing
On thro life he goes;
Each morning sees some work begun,
Each evening sees it close,"—
But he has all the grit,
Tho' his tum-tum may be sair,
For another year is coming,
With its castles in the air.
Tho fortune may not smile,
Upon his labors here
There is a world above,
Where his prospects will be clear—
If he now accepts the offer,
Of a stake beyond compare—
A happy home for all,
With a castle in the air.

Words by James Anderson, Williams Creek, 7th May 1867, *Cariboo Sentinel*
Tune: Traditional
Arrangement: Richard Wright
Richard Wright, vocals; Ken Hamm, guitar; John Law, mandolin; Michele Law, bass

Bastion, Fort Victoria

Chief Douglas's Daughter

When Charles Good and Alice Douglas eloped from Vancouver Island to Port Townsend, Washington Territory, in 1861, they provided the kind of delicious scandal that makes tabloid headlines today.

Alice was the daughter of James Douglas, Hudson's Bay Company governor and the first Governor of the Colony of British Columbia. Charles, a Cambridge graduate, was Douglas's private secretary. He was not the Governor's first choice for the hand of his seventeen-year-old daughter. When the secretary dared ask for Alice's hand, Douglas punched him in the eye.

On August 28th, the pair slipped aboard the *Explorer* and sailed through international waters to the U.S., where they were married by a justice of the peace. The *Colonist* of August 30, 1861, reported, "It seems that the clerk left the harbor on Wednesday afternoon in the schooner *Explorer*, ostensibly for a pleasure trip on the Sound; but after reaching Beacon Hill the vessel laid off and on until dark, when he came ashore in a small boat, and proceeding to the residence of his betrothed's father, watched an opportunity after the family had retired to rest to meet and escort the young lady to the schooner and then up sail for the American side."

When Douglas realized they were gone, he sent W. M. T. Drake in pursuit. The unhappy solicitor was himself romantically interested in Alice, but his hopes were dashed. By the time he caught up with them, they were legally married.

The next report appears September 2, 1861, announcing the marriage of the second son of Rev. Henry Good and the fourth daughter of His Excellency James Douglas, at Christ Church, Victoria. The ceremony on August 31st was performed by Rev. Charles Cridge. This second wedding solemnized before God, the HBC and witnesses the marriage begun so precipitously.

Alice Douglas

Charles Good

Governor Douglas and his wife, Amelia, typified the race relations of the early days of the country's colonization by Europeans. Douglas was born in the West Indies, son of a Scot who was part of the Glasgow sugar industry and of a Creole woman. Amelia was daughter of a Hudson's Bay Company Chief Factor, William Connelly, and his common-law Cree wife. Although Connelly left her to marry a white woman, the Supreme Court of Canada declared the marriage valid in 1869, a move that eased Amelia's passage into Victoria's upper-crust society.

James Douglas was already HBC governor when he assumed the mantle of colonial governor. He realized that miners would soon pour across the border and it would be necessary to establish British sovereignty over the claims, but there was no legislative body, no person or body of authority. As the sole west coast British authority, Douglas, based on the Australian example, assumed that role until such time as someone was appointed.

On December 28, 1857, he issued a proclamation that Fraser and Thompson River gold belonged to the Crown and announced a system of mining licenses to be instituted in February 1858, the fee to be twenty-two shillings, five dollars American. Anyone removing gold without authorization would "be prosecuted, both criminally and civilly, as the law allows." He had moved just in time. By March 1858 newspapers were spreading the gold excitement in sensational front-page stories. By mid-summer ten thousand men had headed up the Fraser River, in search of gold. The rush was on, Douglas's place in history assured.

As to Secretary Good, whatever his ambitions may have been when he joined the staff of Governor Douglas, his star rose in the company of this important family. He became clerk in the Legislative Assembly and went on to the post of Deputy Provincial Secretary. The jilted suitor, Drake, was elected to the colony's Legislative Council and reared a family with a wife more responsive to his attentions.

The star-crossed lovers of fairy tales live happily ever after. This was not to be the case with Charles Good and Alice Douglas. At some point they divorced. Later records show that Good returned to England alone in 1877 and that both eventually remarried.

In the song the young couple sailed from Victoria on Vancouver Island to Port Townsend, in what is now Washington State. They struck a double blow to social mores. Not only did they not have the permission of young Alice's father, they also fled to a foreign country where they could be wed outside the legal jurisdiction that might have helped Douglas stop them.

The Eagles in the first and second verses are $20 gold pieces. The U.S. currency was in common use on both sides of the border.

Theatre Royale, Government Street, Victoria

In the fourth verse, the writer links Sir Frances Drake, the first English explorer to circumnavigate the globe, in 1577-80, to the *Explorer,* the name of the schooner that is spiriting Alice away.

Alice swears "by the rood," an old word for the cross. The "JP" who ended the couple's troubles in the sixth verse was the justice of the peace who performed the wedding ceremony, allowing Alice to say in the seventh verse that she is married "Yankee Fashion."

Drake was "brailing up the spanker" when he caught sight of the errant pair. Victoria musician and sailor Paddy Hernon explains the term this way: "The spanker is a small gaff-headed sail on the aftermost mast of a bark, or barque, if you prefer. In other words, a little sail out the back of the boat. Gaff-headed is a sail that has a stick at the top called a gaff. Usually the spanker is raised and lowered as with regular gaff-headed sails, but occasionally, particularly if the sail is loose-footed, that is, there is no boom at the bottom of the sail, the sail will have lines that run out to the luff, the edge of the sail away from the mast. These lines are called brails. With this arrangement, it isn't necessary to drop the sail in order to douse it. Simply by pulling on the brails the sail will be gathered in to the mast. To set the sail again the brails are released and the clew is pulled back with the sheets."

"Jonathan" and "John Bull" in the seventh verse were nicknames for the U.S. and England. The knot tied in haste by "Jonathan" would not have withstood the scrutiny of Victorian society. The second wedding allowed the young couple to be considered properly married.

The eighth verse would have set tongues to wagging. Neither the bedroom nor the intimate activity implied was deemed a suitable topic for public discussion.

Chief Douglas's Daughter is found in A. S. Farwell's manuscript in the B.C. Archives. His "Colonial Jottings" says, "Written by Ben Griffin on the elopement of Miss Douglas with Good." Griffin owned the Boomerang Hotel in Victoria. The End note: "From E Stamp. Dec. 1st 1864," would seem to indicate that Edward Stamp gave the song or words to Farwell.

The song, as pointed out by Phil Thomas in his *Songs of the Pacific Northwest*, is a reworking of the Thomas Campbell ballad, *Lord Ullin's Daughter*, from the turn of the 18th century. This poem was put to the tune of *Pearl of the Irish Nation*, which came from *Charming Fair Eily*. There is more than one version of the tune to be found. Ours is a reworking of Phil Thomas's.

This song, like others in this collection such as *Mary, Come Home,*

Lover's Lament and many of James Anderson's songs, is an example of both an old tune and song being used to construct a new story, a new lyric. Often the words are very similar, with sections of the old being retained. Here the original poem reads:

> A chieftain to the Highlands bound,
> Cries, "Boatman do not tarry!
> And I'll give thee a silver pound
> To row us o'er the ferry!"—
> "Now, who be ye, would cross Lochgyle,
> This dark and stormy weather?"
> "Oh, I'm the chief of Ulva's isle,
> And this, Lord Ullin's daughter."

Many phrases were mirrored, including the last line: "And he was left lamenting."

It is easy to imagine someone who knew the original seeing how it could be made into a song that could be sung down at the pub to get a laugh. The performance on the CD reflects the comic-opera nature of an incident that was an embarrassment to the Douglas family but perfect for the satirist's pen.

Interior, Fort Victoria

Chief Douglas's Daughter

A trav'ler bound across the sound
Cries, "Boatman, do not tarry
And Eagles three I'll give to thee
To row us o'er the Ferry!"
"Now who be ye would cross the flood,
This wild and stormy water?"
"Hush, man, I'm Secretary Good,
And this the Douglas daughter.

"Three days ago I sought her hand
Her Father bade me dry up,
And should he find me where I stand
He'd bung my other eye up."
Out spake the hardy boatman then,
"Come on my buck I am ready.
It is not for your Eagles bright
But for your plucky Lady.

"And by my word the bonny bird
Shall soon find fortune's frowns end
For tho' the waves are raging white
I'll take thee to Port Townsend."
The Chieftain after dinner sat
O'er his rum & water,
"But where's my Alice? Where's my pet,
My daughter, oh my daughter?"

He to his castle window hied.
He gazed out o'er the trellis
And in a schooner bobbing round
Espied his daughter Alice.
"What ho, my gallant Drake," he cried
"Quick to my house restore her.
Of old, your sire explored yon coast.
Go catch me yon '*Explorer*'."

Sir James Douglas

"In stature he exceeds six feet. His countenance, by its weather-beaten appearance, still tells of many years spent in fur-trapping adventure, in the wilds of the interior…The stateliness of his person—of which he always seems proudly conscious—and his natural force of character suggest the reflection to an observer, how vastly more agreeable would have been his character and abilities had he enjoyed in early life a liberal education and intercourse with persons of refinement and culture."
Matthew MacFie,
Vancouver Island and British Columbia, 1865

Lady Amelia Douglas

W. M. T. Drake

Chief Douglas's Daughter

Found in the diary of
A. W. Farwell,
1864, BCARS
Tune: traditional -
public domain
Words: Ben Griffin
Arrangement:
Cathryn Wellner
Cathryn Wellner,
vocals; Ken Hamm,
guitar; Donna
Konsorado, banjo;
John Law,
mandolin; Michele
Law, bass

"Now haste, love, haste," the lady cried.
"Oh Charlie dear I'd rather
Be married on the other side
Than taken back to Father.
And by the rood my sight is good,
That sternmost schooner stuck in,
I'm sure I see that odious Drake.
I hope he will get a ducking."

The night fell dark, the lovers' barque
By Cupid's aid befriended
The land was made, the JP paid
And all their troubles ended.
And in the morn the gallant Drake
While brailing up the spanker
Espied the lovers in a Bay
Quite cosily at anchor.

Quick alongside, impetuously,
He boarded in a passion.
"Come back," said he. "I shan't,"
Said she, "I'm married Yankee fashion."
"Ah, is it so," cried Drake, "alas
None destiny can master.
Since Jonathan has tied you fast
John Bull must tie you faster.

"Come back, it is your sire's command
Tho' all his plans you've blighted
And since you've been united here
You'll there be reunited."
Back then they came and in the church,
Both Pa & Ma consenting,
The pair were wed, went home to bed,
And Drake was left lamenting.

HUTS AND STORES AT ANTLER'S CREEK.

Up by Barkerville

First Nations in the Goldfields

The natives of B.C. were an active part of the gold rush at all levels. They helped miners find gold, fought off invading miners in the Fraser Canyon and the Chilcotin, provided knowledge of the country, became packers, worked on claims and married many of the first Europeans to settle in the country.

The native peoples of the Cariboo goldfields called themselves the Takulli, the "people who go upon the water." When Alexander Mackenzie canoed across the continent in 1792, 12 years before Lewis and Clarke traversed the United States, he met these people and learned of the Grease Trail that led him to the western sea. Simon Fraser followed in 1808, navigating the river that was to bear his name to the sea.

Oral history of some bands still tells the stories of these first whites. One told by the Shuswap people around Soda Creek remembers through three generations that some of the Soda Creek people were about to leave to go west into the Chilcotin when a runner came to the village with news of strange people coming down the river. It was Fraser, heading for the sea.

20

Interior Natives were an active part of B.C. gold rushes

Mackenzie and Fraser and the fur traders who followed, called the tribes of the upper Fraser the "Atnah" or "Carriers," named for a custom surrounding death. When a man died his body was placed on a pyre, and his widow stayed near until forced away by the flames. The bones were later gathered and placed in a bark container that the widow carried on her back during waking hours for one year.

The Takulli were fishermen and like spawning salmon followed the waters of the Bowron River upstream to the chain of lakes where they used weirs and barriers to funnel the fish into baskets. With natural fibres they fashioned dip-nets similar to those still used today by natives on traditional, hereditary fishing rocks.

During the spring and summer months they lived in permanent or semi-permanent villages of rectangular lodges. In fall and winter, when they followed the salmon to lakes such as Bowron, they built villages of dwellings called Keekwillies—semi-subterranean circular pits covered with a conical structure of poles and earth.

One such village was at the Bowron Lake outlet, a site with about ten dwellings that unfortunately slid into the lake as a result of undermining caused by the 1964 Anchorage, Alaska, earthquake. Smaller camps were scattered along the portage trails of the chain.

When the first miners moved into the area in the mid-1800s there were few reports of natives. They no longer fished the lakes or canoed the river. The people had gone.

One of the early miners was Neil Wilson, the "Swamp Angel" or "swampy," a man who moves through the area's history like a fall mist rising from warm water. He was named for his exploration of the upper Cariboo River, called the Swamp River early on. Swampy fished the lakes to augment his prospecting and mining. One ounce of gold bought one sockeye salmon or a dozen rainbow trout. Swampy traveled a country few others saw and on an early trip to Bowron, then Bear, Lake he met an Indian woman who said she was the last of her tribe. The rest of her people were buried on Deadman's Island (now Pavich), killed by smallpox. The sickness was punishment, she said, for the killing of some miners who were prospecting on the Bowron River. If so, it is little wonder that the Takullis abandoned the Bowron and Cariboo rivers in favor of less threatening watercourses. Their fishing grounds were about to be drastically changed by the men who came to dig for gold.

South of the Quesnel River the Carrier territory gave way to the Shuswaps, and west of the Fraser was the stronghold of the Chilcotins. The exact boundaries are still being negotiated.

When Peter Dunleavy and party came up the Fraser and camped at the mouth of the Chilcotin in the spring, he met a Shuswap called Tomah whose cousin Bacheese later led them north from Kamloops to the first gold strike on the Horsefly River. Despite the minor "wars" or skirmishes in the Fraser Canyon, native peoples were soon working for miners as packers and laborers. Many miners, merchants and settlers took native wives. The names Dunleavy, Sellars, Nason, Mason, Bowe, Rohr, Moffat, Brown, Whitecott, English and many more soon spoke of mixed-race marriages. Most of the men stayed with their wives. Some married; others like Joe Mason and Ithiel Nason, deserted them when white women began immigrating into the area.

The First Nations people who worked and lived along the gold creeks came from a variety of bands and areas, some from as far as the U.S. and the coast. Sarah was a Klickitat who may have come north with the early cattle drives; Hyda or Haida Annie was surely from the coast, and "Gentle Annie" sometimes went home to the "salt chuck" (coast).

"Joseph, a Similkameen Indian aged about 30 years," was interred at Richfield by Father McGluckin in 1867. Nellie Boucher, "married" for a time to Ithiel Nason and later a Flynn, was a Carrier Métis from Fort St. James.

White miners seemed to make little attempt to learn native names, or Chinese for that matter, so they became know by nicknames: Haida Annie, Gentle Annie, Full Moon, Lucy Bones, or just a first name like Susan. We have little record of the men or women except when they appear in the newspaper or police records, usually when they had been illegally sold liquor by whites. The same can be said for many Europeans and Americans.

On the other hand, a close look at mining photos shows many native labourers, and we know that the first Hurdy dancers were native women.

Barkerville diaries and newspapers refer to natives going "to the lower country" or the "salt chuck" for winter and returning in the spring. Here the event is remembered from a First Nations' point of view, a window into another time, place and culture.

Augusta Tappage was born in 1888 in the Soda Creek area of B.C.'s Cariboo, the granddaughter of a Shuswap Chief. When she was in her 80s she spoke to Jean Speare about her life. The wonderful book is still in print with Douglas & McIntyre, Vancouver, B.C.

Up by Barkerville - The Lillooets

That was a big cloud of dust 'way down
to the south in the spring, yes.
It was the Lillooet Indians coming north,
coming north to the goldfields
up by Barkerville.

They go north into that country to work,
to work all the time, hard,
horses and wagons, women and children,
and dogs, hiyu dogs, all going
up by Barkerville.

They work from the time they get there
till fall, till the leaves drop, yes,
and the snow comes and it freezes
the lakes and the creeks
up by Barkerville.

It was the Lillooets going by in the spring
with packing horses, packing freight, yes,
into the mines somewhere in the mountains
and into the creeks
up by Barkerville.

All from Lillooet and I see them passing,
they are passing and passing and, no,
I couldn't ask them where they go—
they speak a different language,
but they go up by Barkerville.

We speak Shuswap, all of us Shuswap—
Soda Creek, Sugar Cane, Alkalai, Canoe Creek,
Dog Creek, Canim Lake—all speak Shuswap,
except the Lillooets who go
up by Barkerville.

They come back in the fall, these Lillooets,
tired, I guess, but lots of money, lots of fish,
not minding snow or mud. They laugh
thinking of summer, yes,
up by Barkerville.

Mary Augusta
Tappage, *Days of
Augusta*
Narration: Cathryn
Wellner

This passage is used
with permission of
author Jean Speare.
Jean lives in Quesnel,
an active member of
the Friends of
Barkerville. William
Speare, her late
husband, was in large
part responsible for
Barkerville's being
declared a heritage
site in B.C.'s
Centennial year of
1958.

Do They Miss Me at Home?

S ongs of the mid 1800s fell into several broad categories, including sentimental ballads which were often morality pieces. An example is *Father, Come Home*, which began with the spoken intro: "'Tis the song of Little Mary, standing at the barroom door, while the shameful midnight revel rages wildly as before." Sentimental ballads were often of the sort represented in *Do They Miss Me at Home?*, or they might lament a lost love, who in Stephen Foster's case was usually dead. He seldom wrote of living people.

Another genre was Plantation Ballads, described elsewhere as the "darkey songs" or the "dese, dem and dose" songs. For the most part they are usually no longer sung or the words have been altered.

As the Civil War in the U.S. began and as the death toll climbed, there was a rash of songs about soldiers, generals, fighting, nationalism and separation. Stephen Foster's *When this Dreadful War is Ended*, written in 1863, is an example. If the South came out with a song, the North parodied it or answered it with fervor.

Novelty songs were also popular. *Oh where oh where has my little dog gone* was one or *My Grandfather's Clock* and the several sequels it spawned. *Listen to the Mocking Bird* was another, as was *Goober Peas*.

Song sheets, not to be confused with sheet music, were responsible in a good part for the popularity of songs. Printed song sheets were usually six by eight inches, published by a variety of companies all across North America and Europe. They had the lyrics, or at least an approximation of the original lyrics, a graphic of some kind which on occasion matched the subject of the song, the publisher's name, sometimes the composer and author, seldom the date, and the obligatory fancy border.

These were the new songs, and they traveled rapidly across the continent and were quickly sung in concert halls, parlours, saloons and homes. Thousands of such songs were published. The U.S. Library of Congress, for instance, has a collection of close to 4500, most published between 1850 and 1870.

The original words and the graphics give us a window into a time that is not found in other places. While collections of song sheets have not been found for the Cariboo or B.C., collections of sheet music have. We find that within months the popular songs of the U.S. or eastern Canada were popular in a Victoria saloon, a New Westminster theatre, the Theatre Royal in Barkerville, Lange's Concert Hall in Richfield or a camp in the Kootenays.

~⊶⊷~

Do They Miss Me at Home, with lyrics by Catherine A. Mason and music by S. M. Gannis, was written about 1854. It was very popular during the U.S. Civil War and was still being sung in Barkerville in the 1870s. It seems an appropriate question, whether for a soldier mired in battlefield muck or a miner in cold gravel.

As was common at the time, an answer song was soon published with the title, *Yes, We Miss Thee at Home*, in this case sung to the same tune:

We miss thee at home—yes we miss thee,
  Since the hour we bade thee adieu,
And prayers have encircled thy pathway,
  From anxious hearts loving and true,
That the Savior would guide and protect thee,
  As far from the loved ones you roam,
And whisper, when'er thou wert saddened,
  They miss thee—all miss thee at home.

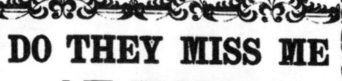

DO THEY MISS ME

AT HOME?

Do they miss me at home? do they miss me?
  'Twould be an assurance most dear,
To know that this moment some loved one
  Were saying I wish he were here!
To feel that the group at the fireside
  Were thinking of me as I roam:
Oh! yes 'twould be joy beyond measure,
  To know that they missed me at home.

When twilight approaches, the season
  That ever is sacred to song,
Does some one repeat my name over,
  And sigh that I tarry so long:
And is there a chord in the music,
  That's missed when my voice is away!
And a chord in each heart that awaketh
  Regret at my wearisome stay?

Do they set me a chair near the the table,
  When evening's home pleasures are nigh,
When the candles are lit in the parlor,
  And the stars in the calm azure sky?
And when the "good nights" are repeated,
  And all lay them down to sleep,
Do they think of the absent and waft me
  A whispered "good night" while they sleep,

Do they miss me at home? do they miss me.
  At morning, at noon, or at night?
And lingers one gloomy shade round them.
  That only my presence can light?
Are joys less invitingly welcome,
  And pleasures less hale than before,
Because one is missed from the circle,
  Because I am with them no more?

THOS G. DOYLE, Bookseller, Stationer, Song Dealer,
&c., No. 297 Gay Street, near Ashland Square, Balt.
☞ORDERS FOR MUSIC PROMPTLY ATTENDED TO.

Cariboo Amateur Dramatic Association, Barkerville

Of a Theatre performance Arthur Bushby wrote: "Rehearsal - Amusing. I'm supposed to accompany. No music and most of the things unknown to me. The fact of the 'Judge' taking his seat at the piano is supposed to suffice! Specimen of my programme. 1. M.F. 6/8 time. 2. in G 3/4 time, etc. Key & time - the rest left to chance."

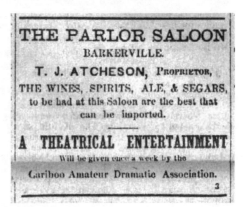

Theatre Royal - The performance by the Amateurs on Saturday evening last for the benefit of Mrs. S. P. Parker was not so well attended as might have been expected. The performance, however, gave entire satisfaction.

Miss Minnie Parker sang "Do They Miss Me At Home?" very sweetly, accompanying herself very tastefully on the piano, and received a rapturous encore, ... with much applause.

Cariboo Sentinel, July 29, 1871

Words: Catherine A. Mason
Music: S.M.Grannis
Arrangement: Cathryn Wellner
Cathryn Wellner, vocals; Willie P. Bennett, harmonica; Ken Hamm, guitar; Caridwen Irvine, fiddle; Donna Konsorado, banjo; John Law, mandolin; Michele Law, harmony vocals, bass; Richard Wright, autoharp

Sheet music sources:
The Lester S. Levy Sheet Music Collection has versions with harmonies .
Authors' collection - Piano arrangement for mixed voices:
Links to sheet music at http://grassrootsgroup.com/sheetmusic.htm

Early days in Yale

Meiss Saloon, Horsefly

Whiskey Dealers & Fallen Angels

"**S**he was a notorious keeper of a house of ill fame and, moreover, on this occasion the wretched woman proved to be intoxicated and I was obliged to request her to go away." This was Johanna Maguire, "soiled dove," resident of Barkerville, Cariboo country, August 1862, as seen by Anglican Bishop George Hills.

"Yet she had done several acts of kindness to the invalid," he added. And there was the angel in Johanna Maguire, the miner's nurse, the daughter of Daniel O'Connell, the great Irish liberator. Maguire is the epitome of the goldrush Fallen Angels, the women who sold whiskey and their bodies to lusty miners, then nursed them through smallpox and typhoid fevers.

Whiskey dealers, gamblers, thieves, prostitutes, madams, pimps and barkeeps followed hard on the heels of any rush for frontier wealth. When miners poured into B.C. from Oregon, California and beyond, the Cariboo was no exception.

Gold drew men and women to the Fraser River frontier of British North America in 1858; and gold enticed them north to the Cariboo in 1860. Keithley's Creek boomed and Harvey's and Cunningham's. On the Cariboo Mountains' north slope they tapped Antler Creek and literally plucked nuggets from the streambed. A pan of gold brought $75, the equivalent of $1,500 today.

But the real Cariboo rush was William's Creek, discovered in 1861 by "Dutch Bill" and his party. The next season Billy Barker and company struck the lead, and fabulous wealth flowed into their hands. Opportunities were not far behind. From Antler Creek to San Francisco the parasites poured in to suck miners dry.

Back in the comforts of Victoria, Bishop Hills could not understand the gold camp's social life.

"The fact is these men, worthy men as miners, are so accustomed to life in the transits of vice, and to hear blasphemy and evil discourse of immorality, that they have sunk to a lower level, depraved...[and they] pronounce excellent and praise to the skies a keeper of a house of ill fame, a drunkard and blasphemer and a prostitute, a wretched woman who happened to show a kind disposition to the sick."

The point of Hills' private tirade is that life in the goldfields was not as refined as history would have us believe. The social rules and barriers that made Bishop Hills and his congregation comfortable had been cast aside.

In Johanna's time, women were few and so filled multiple roles. Those viewed by cultured society as degenerates reverted to the ancient role of mother or nurse when the situation demanded. So a businesswoman like hotelier Big Jennie Allen or Elizabeth Kelly or a prostitute became nurse and angel to an injured miner.

While a few miners' wives and businesswomen drifted north, the majority of women were those who, frequently backed by men's money and protection, feasted at the miner's table. The decades from 1850 to 1870 were difficult for women around the world. Social structure was changing. Wars had decimated the male population; wealthy families were losing money. Women had to find work to stay alive. So they became entrepreneurs or sailed to the colonies on brideships.

Given Victorians' prudish sanctimony, it is not surprising that this gold rush demimonde is poorly documented. Clues surface in letters, diaries, police reports, obituaries and infrequent newspaper articles. Victoria's colonial government struggled to present and preserve the image of British gold towns as law abiding and God fearing, but it is clear from journalists and diarists that they were rough, lively places.

In the summer of 1862 a miner wrote from Williams Creek that, "there is a great deal of gambling and drinking carried on by the lucky miners and on fine days you could see Cypreans [prostitutes] promenading about in long boots, britches and fancy hats."

A Victoria *Colonist* September 1862 article on prostitutes, picked up with alacrity by San Francisco papers, said the prostitutes "on the creek—nine in number...swagger through the saloons...with cigars or huge qwids of tobacco in their mouths...looking like anything but the angels in petticoats heaven intended. Each has a revolver or bowie knife attached to her waist, and it is quite a common occurrence to see one or more women in male attire playing poker in the saloons, or drinking whiskey at the bars."

Having titillated readers and allowed a disgusted "tsk tsk," the editor/reporter then added his Victorian disclaimer. "They are a degraded set, and all good men in the vicinity wish them hundreds of miles away." It is doubtful he was speaking for Cariboo miners. There is little evidence the women were "wished away."

Johanna Maguire left Williams Creek in the fall of 1862, after one season, with $3,000—$45,000 today. She did not earn it washing clothes, nor by being unpopular. Julia Picot paid for her hotel in one year. Reports of a prostitute's death or travels would refer to her being "well-known in the colony."

Liquor flowed freely in over a dozen saloons that ranged from the small whiskey shop of Eliza Bailey to the huge dancing and billiard saloons of Martin & Cook, Barry & Adler and James D. Loring's "Go-at'em Saloon."

Pilsener and lager beers were made on site. Nicolas Cunio had a large brewery for his XXX Pale Ale, as did Kerr and Co. Their barley was grown at Australian Ranch, and by A.S. Bates at 150 Mile. Wine, mostly sparkling varieties, was imported, as was whiskey.

Some Cariboo hooch was called "mountain howitzer or rifle whiskey," guaranteed to kill at 1,000 yards. William Pinchbeck had a distillery at Williams Lake, and over in the Chilcotin Ludwig W. Riske of Riske Creek made 191 gallons of "distilled spirits" between September and December 1865. Saloons also offered reading rooms with the latest papers. There were billiard or carom tables, card games, gambling on horses, and bowling. In 1867 Fenton built a saloon and bowling alley with a remarkable 104-ft. frontage. Raucous music and dancing started at 7 p.m. and lasted until 6 a.m.

James Loring, who made a fortune as partner in the Diller claim, was likely the first to bring in dancing partners for miners. By 1865 he had employed Native women at his Terpsychorean Saloon in Camerontown. From that time on, Native women were part of the dark side of Barkerville's social life, most often surfacing when miners gave them liquor illegally, or as prostitutes like Lucy Bones and Gentle

Annie, and as the common-law wives of merchants such as Ithiel B. Nason and Joe Mason. As society shifted and more white women came into the country, Native wives and children were shunted off to reserves along the Cariboo Road.

The first hurdy-gurdy saloons were opened in the spring of 1865. By autumn four "sets" of four girls each were whirling on the dance floor and hustling drinks. The rollicking hurdies were brought in from Germany or San Francisco by entrepreneurial saloon owners like Loring or Black Jack Martin. Accounts say they were under the control or protection of a "boss hurdy" who acted as booking agent for a slice of their income. Saloon owners most often took that role.

> In the winter Martin's saloon was the sight of some "rare games, Martin guv a ball down to the saloon thar' and all the boys roun' attended of course."
>
> Ladies? "Oh why we didn hev none, 'cept old Nigger Mary' (a fat negress who did washing for the miners) an' the French madam, an the blacksmith's wife. But we danced som I tell yu! it were stag dancing of course, fur a hundred an fifty men was too many fur three females, but it came off all gay, till some rg'lar skunk when an' put croton ile in the pastry, an' then I reckon after supper some of us was a bit queer fur a while."
>
> Winter of 62/63
> R. Byron Johnson, *Very Far West Indeed*

John Milross was an exception. He appears in early Barkerville as a bartender who supplemented his income with sign painting. By the 1870s he was "boss" of "Milross' Hurdy's" whom he hustled between Barkerville and Lightning Creek when neither town could support a full-time dancing set. The Austins also "bossed" a set of hurdies at the Stanley Hotel in the early '70s.

There is no clear evidence that hurdies were prostitutes and little that they weren't. Their contract was for three years, when return passage would be paid to Germany or San Francisco, but many stayed to marry miners or merchants. Best known were Jeanette and Magge Ceise, sisters who married John Houser [Hauser] and Charles House.

Charles House was a well-known Barkerville "sport" or gambler, once charged with keeping an illegal faro game in a saloon. He went into the saloon business with his friend Joe Denny and fell in love with dancer Magge Ceise, one of the last hurdies to dance in Barkerville or Stanley. They were married July 31, 1876. A decade later Magge bought the House Hotel. The two sisters lived the rest of their lives in Barkerville.

Other hurdies who stayed included Katrina Mundorf, of 124 Mile House at Bonaparte. She divorced Jacob Mundorf after years of abuse. Elizabeth Ebert married Edward Dougherty and went to live at Maiden Creek. Angelo Pendola married a hurdy named Martha Lursden, moved to Kamloops and opened the Savona Brewery. Charlotte Millington tried to forget she was a dancing girl. After she and husband R. H. Brown moved to Victoria, she was known as a former governess and mid-wife.

Dancing was not the only dalliance in saloons. Apartments off the dance floor were used for sexual dalliances. No prostitute or customer left a diary, but some names have been passed down in police records.

Mary Sheldon, Mary Nathan and Annie Miller were all brothel madams. They frequently traveled with other women such as Miss Kitty and Miss Lizzie by stagecoach down to Yale, perhaps on a brothel circuit, similar to those in California.

Hattie Lucas was fined for sticking a pistol in a butcher's face and whacking him with a "shooting stick," a cane gun, after an argument. Described as a "woman of the town...tall and graceful young woman, having considerable personal attraction," she was in a knock-down fight with Welsh miner and ne'er-do-well William Williams.

Sophie Rouillard drifted in from history. She was born in Calais, France, and was likely an Ingot, part of the great French migration following the Lottery of the Golden Ingots. This French government scheme to send riff-raff to North America dumped thousands of French criminals in California. Some wandered north.

Rouillard arrived in Barkerville in spring 1868 and quickly went into business. Apparently she had money, for she loaned Caesar Cassier $500. When she asked for repayment for the third time, Cassier punched her hard in the stomach. "That blow will be the death of me," she told him. Her stomach was "on fire" for days, but even Dr. Bell couldn't help. Ten days later she died in her house. The law was on the side of men. The inquest jury of 12 men, four of whom held liquor licenses, found she died by "the visitation of God in a natural way, accelerated by the use of strong drink, and not otherwise." Sophie was 25 years old.

Juries were consistent. When a Chinese prostitute died in a "house of ill fame," with Solomon-like wisdom they returned a verdict of "found dead." When Chinese prostitutes were sold or hustled to another town, the only concern was whether a colonial law had been broken.

Williams Creek gold and miners' sweat supported all the high-priced businesses of Williams Creek. It was not just the whiskey dealers and fallen angels that sucked a miner's money away. Merchants charged enormous prices for goods. The government taxed everything. The average daily wage was $4 to $10. A dance with the hurdies cost $1, a drink 25 cents. What the freighters, merchants, saloons and government didn't take, the doctors might. A minor visit was $10. For a death inquest, the sawbones received $25.

The Colonial government's attitude was that if you paid a tax or licence and kept your drunkenness and debauchery behind closed doors, everything was okay. Public drunkenness, whether lawyer Joseph Park or Native woman Annie Pagguet, was unacceptable. Yet only two charges were laid for keeping a brothel or disorderly house.

Most gold rush women faded into history or the anonymity of their husband's name. Some went back to California. A few stayed on in Barkerville, like the notorious Mary Nathan who died there in 1878 and lies in an unmarked grave.

These folks and their stories are the dark side of our history, but, finally, as important to British Columbia's story as the Judge Begbies, Billy Barkers and Bishop Hills.

In James Anderson's 1864 letter, where he speaks of women on the creek (the following narration), he says, "Each ane's [one's] a mistress, too ye'll find, to make guid folks think that she's joined in honest wedlock unto one."

Here Anderson is referring to the gold rush practice of taking on different names. Women often borrowed the name of a male friend or simply added Mrs. to their name, sometimes in an effort to appear married, sometimes to avoid recognition. Eliza Ord was known as Mrs. Bailey for a time, but in California was Mrs. Christian.

Men did the same, more commonly becoming known only by a nickname, such as Chips, or Doc, or Blue Dick, Billy the Bladge, Red Alick. This gave rise to the song, "What was your name in the States?" It also spawned the folkloric story told in every gold rush of a man searching for his brother, whom he did not find because he did not know his nickname.

> Oh, what was your name in the States,
> Was it Thompson or Johnson or Bates,
> Did you flee for your life,
> Or murder your wife?
> Say, what was your name in the States?

There are some women on this creek (narration)

There are some women on this creek,
Sae modest, and sae mild and meek!
The deep red blush aye pents their cheek,
They never swear, but when they speak,
Each ane's a mistress, too, ye'll find,
To mak guid folks think that she's joined
In honest wedlock unto one;
"She's your, or any other man's!"
But dinna fear, for me at least,
I'll never mak mysel' a beast!
But let this drap—"to err is human,"
An' Fraility, thy name is woman."
    James Anderson, Sawney's Letters,
    February 1864

James Anderson,
    Sawney's Letters,
    February 1864
Narration: Duncan Bell

Related songs and narrations:
Erin's green shore
Mary Come Home
The German Lasses
There are some women
The way they dance in
    this country
Dancing Gals of Cariboo

> Dere's de Dush gals, dey's purty smart gals, mister editer, to hold down dere own in dis country, poor gals, I hope dey may continy to do so; de stokeepers is offul down on 'em cos dey krell all de dimes, bully for de gals, dey's on it, you bet, on de make I means, sar. De sloon keepers, dere offul down on de gals too, coss dey draw de boys, and draw de dollars; but de sloon keepers oughter know dat de dance galls aluss took better dan anyting else in Californey, de meenus man will spen a dollar dor a dance, coss "him dearly lubs de lasses, O."
> Dixie, [Isaac Dickson] *Cariboo Sentinel*, June 12, 1865

Pioneer Cemetery, Quadra Street, Victoria

Erin's Green Shore
Joanna Maguire

This song is a linchpin of British Columbia history and folklore, the link between documented fact, folklore and music, between the old world and the colonies, the upper-crust courts and the gutters of a young frontier. It is the stuff of which our history is made.

Johanna Maguire, born about 1829, appears on the B.C. stage in 1858 in Yale and later as a Barkerville prostitute. She appears in Bishop Hills's journal of 1862, the *British Colonist* newspaper, D. W. Higgins's stories and Robert Stevenson's reminiscences. In Yale she received a monthly stipend from Dublin. Higgins wrote that, "One morning a tall, dissipated-looking woman, very plainly draped, entered the place and enquired if there were any letters for Johanna Maguire."

The postal clerk told Higgins it was postmarked Dublin. He said they always contained a 5£ note. Johanna, said Higgins, had two voices, one a broad Irish accent, habitually profane. But he also heard her speak to a sick child in a soft, cultured voice, reciting the Lord's prayer. "That woman wears a mask," said Higgins.

Stevenson refers to her as, "the once Irish lady of the city of Dublin. She was undoubtedly the lost daughter of Dan O'Connell, the great Irish liberator. *So she is referred to in Irish song.* Her name was Johanna McGuire [*sic*]. We had the proof right there in Cariboo. A brother of an Irish peer told Judge Cox, Sir Matthew Begbie [Judge], the late Judge Walkem, Murdoch Campbell and myself that he was well acquainted with her and had met her frequently in society in Dublin." [Editor's emphasis]

O'Connell, known in Irish political history as the "Liberator," played a significant role in Ireland's development by spearheading the Catholic Emancipation, posing a formidable force against the British occupation.

Johanna was in Barkerville and Richfield, where she owned property, during the summer of 1862. Bishop Hills wrote of her in his diary of Sunday August 10, 1862, when he refers to a woman who is visiting a sick miner.

"I found out however from themselves that she was a notorious keeper of a house of ill fame and moreover on this occasion the wretched woman proved to be intoxicated and I was obliged to request her to go away. The sick man was much troubled at her intrusion in such a state. Yet she had done several acts of kindness to the invalid."

The miners were so accustomed to a life of vice, said Hills, that they "could pronounce excellent and praise to the skies a keeper of a house of ill fame, a drunkard & blasphemer and prostitute, a wretched woman who happened to show a kind disposition to the sick. Her name was Johanna."

She left with $3000, not earned by washing shirts or mending clothes. When she was lost on the trail for a few days the *British Colonist* reported: "Johanna Maguire, the Cariboo cyprian reported murdered and robbed has returned to life." Her money and horse were lost.

In Victoria she fell in with Edward Whitney and lived in a small house on Government Street. He frequented the saloons, but Johanna evidently had withdrawn and spent most of her time alone. Her health was failing rapidly. In November 1864 a neighbour called doctors to Johanna's house, where she was found severely beaten, by Whitney—not the first time—but on this occasion she was admitted to the Royal Hospital. Here, according to Higgins, she confided in a lawyer named Kelly, who would only say that "in early life she had been a welcome visitor at Dublin Castle, and that she was connected with one of the highest families in Dublin, a family with an historical record and a lineage that dated back several centuries. Her brogue and rude manners were to conceal her identity."

Whoever she was in her earlier life remained a secret when she died the next day, December 3, 1864. Whitney was held awaiting a trial for murder.

It never happened. At the inquest Dr. Trimble testified his autopsy found that all of her internal organs, including the brain, were in a soft, deteriorating condition. "I believe ... intemperance brought her to the diseased condition." Trimble felt she would have survived the beating and that the actual cause of death was apoplexy, a stroke.

The coroner "did not feel there was any occasion to prosecute the enquiry any further." The all-male jury found that Johanna McGuire's "death ensued from an effusion of blood in the brain."

Johanna was 35. She is buried in the Old Anglican Burial Ground in Victoria, B.C., at Quadra and Meares Street, in an unmarked grave.

Research has not proven that Johanna was a daughter of Daniel O'Connell, who was born 1775 and died 1847, when Johanna would have been 18. If she was it seems certain she was illegitimate, and that could have meant her banishment with an allowance. On one hand sources indicate O'Connell was promiscuous with many mistresses, while others argue this was a view promoted by the British press in attempts to defame him.

The song, with a variety of tunes from *Rosin the Beau, Lily of the West* and *Blooming Bright Star of Belle Isle* to this version, is sung from Newfoundland to Kentucky. It is found in many collections in England and Ireland but has found a particular niche in the oral traditions of Canadian Maritime Provinces and Appalachia. One version is in *Ballads and Sea Songs of Newfoundland*, by Elisabeth Bristol Greenleaf, 1968, as "Erin's Green Shore." In Keith Peacock's 1965 *Songs of Newfoundland Outports* and John H. Cox's *Folk-Songs of the South* it is know as "The Irish Dream." The song follows the dream theme that is common in many ballads: man dreams of woman, man speaks to woman, woman is beautiful, woman gives message, woman disappears, man wakes.

The question could be raised as to where Robert Stevenson heard the song *Erin's Green Shore* and how he knew it was about Johanna Maguire, particularly given the oral tradition associated with the piece. The song is indeed in the oral tradition, but that may be because it was a broadside ballad, published in "song sheet" format, widely distributed in the mid 1800s. A copy is preserved in the U.S. Library of Congress. It is likely from this source that Stevenson knew the song and likely the gossip of Johanna spread through the colonial civil service in B.C.

The obvious questions that remain are why the song specifically refers to Daniel O'Connell, why and when the song's subject was sent from England to Ireland or Canada, and what brought Johanna Maguire from Ireland to be hidden and die on the British Columbia frontier.

Most versions of this song are similar, with verses and lines sometimes transposed and the odd word lost or misquoted. The version we use is from the singing of Patrick Lewis in Newfoundland, 1929, documented in Greenleaf's *Ballads and Sea Songs*, with a nod to Mrs. John Fogarty's 1952 version in Peacock's book, which fit Johanna's B.C. story. It is also very similar to the song sheet.

Published by Johnson, the Great Song Publisher,
No. 7 North Tenth Street, Philadelphia.

ERIN'S GREEN SHORE.

One evening so late as I rambled
   Near the foot of a clear pearling stream;
On a bed of soft primroses
   I slowly began for to dream.
I dreamed I saw a fair female,
   And her equal I had ne'r seen before,
And she sighed for the wrongs of her country,
   As she strayed along Erin's Green Shore.

I gently embraced this fair female,
   My jewel, pray tell me your name,
For I am here in the midst of all danger,
   Or I would never ask you the same.
I am the daughter of Daniel O'Connell,
   And from England I lately sailed over,
For to awaken my brethren,
   As they slumber on Erin's Green Shore.

Her eyes were like two sparkling diamonds,
   Or a star on a cold frosty night,
Her cheeks were like two blooming roses,
   And her skin of an ivory white.
She resembled some goddess of Freedom,
   And green was the mantle she wore,
For it was trimmed with the rose and the shamrock,
   As she strayed on Erin's Green Shore.

In transports of joy I awoke,
   And lo! it was naught but a dream,
For this beautiful damsel had left me,
   And I longed for to slumber again,
May the Heavens above be her guardian,
   For her equal I neer shall see more,
May the sunbeams of freedom shine o'er her, .
   As she strays along Erin's Green Shore.

JOHNSON'S CHEAP PRINTING OFFICE,
NO. 7 NORTH TENTH ST, PHILADA. .

Erin's Green Shore

One evening for pleasure I rambled
On the banks of a clear purling stream.
I sat down on a bed of primroses
And quickly fell into a dream.
I dreamed I beheld a fair maiden
Her equal I'd ne'er seen before,
And she sighed for the woes of her country
As she strolled along Erin's green shore.

Her cheeks were like two blooming roses.
Her teeth were like ivory so white.
Her eyes were two sparkling diamonds
Or the stars on a cold frosty night.
She resembled the goddess of Liberty,
And freedom was the mantle she wore,
Bound round with shamrock and roses
That grew along Erin's green shore.

I quickly addressed this fair damsel,
"My jewel, come tell me your name.
I know in this place you're a stranger
Or ne'er would have asked you the same."
"I know you're a true son of Erin,
My secrets to you I'll unfold.
I am here in the midst of all danger
Not knowing my friend or my foe.
I'm the daughter of Daniel O'Connell
From England I lately sailed o'er.
I came here to awaken my brother,
Who's slumbering on Erin's green shore."

Transported with joy I awakened
And found it was only a dream.
For to see this fair damsel beside me
I longed for to slumber again.
May the heavens above be her guardian,
I know I won't see her no more,
May the sunbeams of glory shine upon her
As she sails along Erin's green shore.

Traditional
Arrangement: Ken
   Hamm and Richard
   Wright
Ken Hamm, vocals,
   guitar; Caridwen
   Irvine, fiddle;
   Donna Konsorado,
   banjo; John Law,
   mandolin; Michele
   Law, bass; Cathryn
   Wellner, harmony
   vocals

Sheet Music Sources:
Various melody line
versions can be found
in *Ballads and Sea
Songs of
Newfoundland*,
Elisabeth Bristol
Greenleaf, Folklore
Associates Inc., 1968,
as "Erin's Green
Shore"; *Songs of
Newfoundland
Outports*, Keith
Peacock, 1865; *Folk-
Songs of the South*,
John H. Cox, where it
is known as "The
Irish Dream."

Barkerville in winter

Mary, Come Home
The Language of the Goldfields

*L*isten to any esoteric, closed group of people and you will hear a distinct language pattern, a jargon that not only enhances and defines the ideas and language but separates the initiated and keeps outsiders at bay. An advertising executive talking in terms of "target audience," rubber-tired market" and "upscale markets" is in part saying, "If you do not understand, you are not one of us."

The same can be said of a pile of placer miners at the Northwoods in Wells, a load of loggers at the Williams Lake Husky, a bonspiel of curlers or a hose-bed full of firefighters. Each part of a country develops speech patterns, accents, expressions and phrases distinct to that area. Western Canada is no exception, with words like: skookum, go-fer, mowitch, saltchuck, cheechako, or gut wrench used in more-or-less everyday language.

Gold rush Cariboo was no exception. Men and women from around the world were mixed together with the creeks' waters and placer gravel and developed a slang that was remarked on by more than one journalist or chronicler. Some of these gold rush expressions are commonplace today, while others have faded into obscurity.

42

Dr. Cheadle and Viscount Milton came to British Columbia in 1863, basically on an extended journey to escape the boredom that was sweeping the well-to-do English of the 1860s. At a roadhouse in Lillooet, Cheadle remarked, "our ears became familiarized with such phrases as 'bully for you,' 'caved-in,' 'played out, or; 'you bet,' 'you bet your life,' 'your bottom dollar,' or 'bet your gumboots on it.'"

Remember that betting and gambling were extremely popular pastimes with miners and "gumboots," at a cost of $50 or five to ten days' wages, were indeed almost as valuable as your life.

Cheadle continued with "'on the make,' ' on the sell,' 'a big strike,' 'can't get a show,' 'hit a streak,' and so on."

Jargon extended to blasphemy. In his book Vancouver Island and British Columbia, Matthew Macfie said, "Profane language is almost universal, and is employed with diabolical ingenuity. The names of 'Jesus Christ' and the 'Almighty' are introduced in most blasphemous connections. Going to church is known among many as 'the religious dodge,' which is said to be 'played out,' or in other words, a superstition which has ceased to have any interest for enlightened members of society."

Macfie continues, explaining that "the slang in vogue in the mining regions is imported mainly from California, and is often expressive as it is original. 'Guessing' and 'calculating' are exercises of perpetual occurrence. If one have the best of a bargain, he is said to have got 'the dead wood' on the other party. A mean and greedy man is 'on the make;' and where a claim is to be disposed of, the proprietor is 'on the sell.' A conceited man thinks himself 'some pumpkins;' and when any statement is made, the exact truth of which is doubted, it is said to be 'rayther (*sic*) a tall story.' When a claim disappoints those interested, it has 'fizzled out.' Credit is 'jaw-bone;'...The ground of the allusion is evident, the product result from the motion of the jaw being the only security a needy purchaser has to offer. Another expression for wanting credit is 'shooting off the face.' Deceit in business is 'shenanigan.' A good road, steamboat, plough, dinner or anything else is 'elegant.' When one has run off to avoid paying his debts, he has 'skedaddled,' or 'vamoosed the ranch.'...When two parties are playing into each others' hands, with a sinister object in view, it is a case of 'log-rolling.'"

Chinook, heard in some of Anderson's songs and poems and in *Mary, Come Home* is argued by some recent scholars as being a language rather than a jargon. And while it was once thought to have been a language invented to ease European and Native trade there is now considerable evidence that it was first a trade language used by the many tribes or language groups of the Pacific Northwest, long before the Europeans landed. The Scots, English, French and Chinese newcomers expanded this language with other words until it had a large vocabulary with a simple grammar.

Many of the terms used in Chinook in the 1800s, such as klootchman, a female native, or Siwash, for a native, were not meant to be derogatory but were part of everyday speech. The fact that words like tum-tum are used by Anderson, as well as the words used in *Mary, Come Home* and those in the *Cariboo Sentinel*, would seem to indicate that most miners had a least a rudimentary understanding of perhaps a few dozen or more words. Some clearly had a good command of the language.

Chinook and the emerging jargon of the goldfields made for a rich language that left cheechakos, visitors and journalists shaking their heads trying to translate the esoteric phrases.

Is modern speech as colorful? Listen to miners, loggers and ranchers in Cariboo or fisher folk in Newfoundland. Compare with those you know 'at the coast' or in "the big smoke." You bet your gumboots it is.

With this in mind *Mary, Come Home* is a good song to view closely in terms of what "Mosquito" is really saying and what it tells us about the years during which it was written.

This song was written in Barkerville about a Mosquito Creek woman, who judging from the Chinook words was likely Mary Bent, a native woman. Mary Bent, aka Stablewis or Betsy, was in Mosquito Creek and Barkerville from 1869 to 1878.

Mosquito was a town that grew up several miles northwest of Barkerville, near the present town of Wells, following a strike by Joseph Trevethick. For a time it was called Centreville. At the time this song was written, it was a new town with a rough road connecting it to the towns on Williams Creek. Wagons and sleighs or "Shank's mare," *i.e.*, walking, connected the towns, for few miners had the luxury of a horse.

In the first verse it appears "Mosquito" is in one of the Williams Creek towns as he says, "the sleigh from Mosquito has come," as he coaxes Mary to come home with him. Clearly this is a winter song and the fact that the author is wintering here likely makes him a partner or owner of a claim. He is not too broke to leave, given his promises and accommodation.

Mosquito Creek, 1868, Hocking Co. claim in foreground

"Mosquito" seems to be one of the prosperous miners. He has a cabin or house built with milled lumber. He is not in a brush tent, a canvas tent, a rooming house or a log cabin, all of which were more common. Also he has the money and the inclination to paper the walls and has a real bed. Mary, it appears, could make a worse choice. Her suitor is successful and lonely.

In the second verse, George is the express driver, ready to leave with his horse [*kiuatan*] drawn sleigh. "Mosquito," generous as he is, is not really keen for Mary to drink "old Tom," a more expensive whiskey but would prefer the locally produced lager beer. "Old Tom" was likely a bourbon and is usually listed separately from whiskey and Scotch.

"Mosquito" says, "I've brought you a message from Yaco." Yaco was Susan Yako, who, judging by the company she usually kept, was a Barkerville prostitute in the early 1870s. Whether this message is the Chinook phrase that follows, or whether the phrase is spoken by Mary, is unclear but Yaco could be encouraging Mary to go with Mosquito with the phrase, "Promise me you'll really come." The phrase *Kloshe waw-waw delate mika chako* is translated as "Tell me truly you'll return," or "Promise you'll really come."

The last verse tells us little more but does indicate the raw, rough clearing that was the town of Mosquito when Mary stops at a stump for a rest. Photos show that at this time Mosquito was a field of stumps. The final line of Chinook *Delate nika chako tomollo*—can be translated as,"I promise I'll come tomorrow"; "I'll really come tomorrow"; or "Truly I'll come tomorrow."

The Chinook phrases in *Mary, Come Home* can be translated in several similar ways. In the song, they had to scan and fit the music. Two Chinook scholars translated the words, here written with their accepted spelling, as follows:

Kiuatan – horse

The phrase *Kloshe waw-waw delate mika chako* is translated as
"Tell me truly you'll return"; or "Promise you'll really come."

Delate nika chako tomollo – "I promise I'll come tomorrow";
"I'll really come tomorrow;" "Truly I'll come tomorrow."

The important difference in the two phrases is the words *mika* and *nika*. *Mika* is you or yours and *nika* is I or me.

The words found in the *Cariboo Sentinel*, Feb. 13, 1869, did not include a chorus. We have added one here based on the chorus of *Come Home, Father*.

Mary, Come Home

Oh, Mary, dear Mary, come home with me now;
The sleigh from Mosquito has come.
You promised to live in my little board house
As soon as the pap'ring was done.
The fire burns brightly in the sheet-iron stove
And the bed is made up by the wall.
But it's lonesome, you know, these long winter
  nights
With no one to love me at all.

Chorus:
Come home, come home, come home.
Please Mary, dear Mary, come home.
Hear the sad voice of this poor miner sing
Which the night winds repeat as they roam,
Oh! Who could resist this most plaintive of
  prayers,
Please Mary, Dear Mary, come home.

Oh, Mary, dear Mary, come home with me now;
Old George with his *kiuatan* is here.
You can, if you like, have your drink of old
  Tom,
But I'd rather you'd drink lager beer.
I've come all this way through the cold drifting
  snow,
And brought you a message from Yaco;
And these were the very last words that she
  said:
"Kloshe waw-waw delate mika chako"
  Chorus

Oh, Mary, dear Mary, come home with me now;
The time by the watch, love, is three.
The night it grows colder, and George with the
  sleigh
Down the road now is waiting for me.
She stopped at a stump on her way up the hill
And whispered for me not to follow;
But pressing my hand ere I left her, she said,
"Delate nika chako tomollo."
  Chorus

Words : "Mosquito," *Cariboo Sentinel* February 13, 1869, a take-off of and music from Henry C. Work's *Come Home, Father,* 1864.

Arrangement and chorus: Richard Wright

Richard Wright, vocals; Ken Hamm, harmony vocals, guitar; Donna Konsorado, banjo; Caridwen Irvine, fiddle; John Law, harmony vocals, mandolin; Michele Law, harmony vocals, bass; Jerry Paquette, harmony vocals

Sheet music sources:
"Come Home, Father"—The Lester S. Levy Sheet Music Collection has versions with harmonies.
Links to sheet music at http:// grassrootsgroup.com/ sheetmusic.htm

The German Lasses

In North America the Hurdy-Gurdys are known primarily as dancehall girls in mining communities. The name, however, comes from a stringed instrument (see illustration above) played with buttons and a wheel that rubs a string, creating a drone, a sound unlike any other instrument. The hurdy-gurdy and the bagpipes were the most popular instruments for dancing in the rural areas of Europe for centuries and were particularly popular in West Germany in the 19th century, where many of the players were young women.

At this time a lack of wars, famines or epidemics and the resulting increase in population meant that farm families could no longer support all their children. The dispossessed wandered and sold wicker products and found that music increased sales. In autumn these Landgänger returned to their communities.

The Landgänger traveled throughout Europe and went on to England, Australia and North America and other lands, under an agent called "the seller of souls." The girls, often called hurdy-gurdy girls, were forced by their agents to work in dancehalls and coffeehouses of seaports, and later the mining camps.

In the Cariboo most of the hurdies were German. They danced in sets of four in the bars, charging for the dance and for their drinks. Many stayed in B.C. and married merchants and miners.

Many of the Cariboo Hurdy Gurdies can now be identified. Women such as Margaret Shaw, Charlotte [Millington] Brown, the Schwitzer sisters, the Ceise sisters, (later House and Houser) Rosa [Haub] Langell and many more came and danced and stayed.

In a letter to historian Louis Lebourdais in the 1930s Jessie (likely Jessie Kibbee) wrote a note saying, "Mother said that Mrs. Mundorf was the one called the Kangaroo and Mrs. Dougherty was 'dumpy little Lizzie, oh!'"

Catherine Elizabeth Haub, "a strappin' rattlin' hizzie," was born in Germany in 1844 and came to Barkerville in 1865 to dance at Jacob Mundorf's Crystal Palace Saloon. They had their first child in December 1867. After four children they were married, perhaps as an ultimatum before they moved south to 20 Mile House a few miles

Thought to be Rosa Haub

south of Clinton. In 1894 Elizabeth sued for divorce, charging physical abuse. Rosa Haub [Langell] was likely Elizabeth's sister.

Mrs. Dougherty was Elizabeth Ebert, born in Holland in 1852. She danced for about two years before marrying Edward Dougherty in 1871 and settling on Maiden Creek just south of Clinton, B.C.

Anderson wrote most of his poems and songs in a Scots dialect. This and the fact that most of his writing is in rhyme has meant much of his interpretation of the early years on the creeks has been overlooked by scholars.

Most of the dialect can be translated easily enough although Anderson may have been adding a double entendre, as hurdies is a Scots word for buttocks.

Anderson wrote this song in March 1866 and based it on *Green Grow the Rashes, O*, by Robert Burns, not to be confused with *Green Grow the Rushes*. In Sawney's letters he says, "The name I've gied's 'The German Lasses.' The air's the same's 'Green Grow the Rashes.'"

Many of Anderson's lines not only echo Burns but mirror them, such as the first two lines, that are virtually the same.

The German Lasses

"There's naught but care on ilka han',
  On every hour that passes, O!"
An' Sawney, man, we hae nae chance
  To spark amang the "lasses", O!

A warldly race that riches chase,
  Yet a'gangs tapselteerie, O!
An' every hour we spent at e'en,
  Is spent without a dearie, O!

Last summer we had lassies here
  From Germany—the hurdies, O!
And troth I wot, as I'm a Scot,
  They were the bonnie hurdies, O!

There was Kate and Mary, blithe and airy,
  And dumpy little Lizzie, O!
And ane they ca'd the Kangaroo,
  A strappin' rattlin' hizzy, O!

They danced at nicht in dresses light,
  Frae late until the early, O!
But oh! their hearts were hard as flint,
  Which vexed the laddies sairly, O!

The dollar was their only love,
  And that they lo'ed fu' dearly, O!
They dinna care a flea for men,
  Let them coort hooe'er sincerely, O!

They left the creek wi' lots of gold,
  Danced frae oor lads sae clever, O!
My blessin's on their "sour krout" heads,
  Gif they stay awa for ever, O!

CHORUS—Bonnie are the hurdies, O!
  The German hurdy-gurdies, O!
    The daftest hour that ere I spent,
  Was dancin' wi' the hurdies, O!

From Letter II, written March, 1866
Sawney's Letters and Cariboo Rhymes by
James Anderson

Words: James Anderson, March 1866
Tune: Green Grow the Rashes, O! Traditional, sometimes credited to Robbie Burns.
Arrangement: Duncan Bell and Jack Velker
Duncan Bell, vocals; Jack Velker, pump organ

Sheet music sources:
Authors' collection - Piano arrangement for mixed voices: http://grassrootsgroup.com/sheetmusic.htm

NOTE
The percussive sounds heard on this track are not a drum or dancing. The sound comes from the pedals on a 120-year-old pump organ with leaking bellows, with Jack Velker turning a problem into a percussion opportunity.

The Dancing Gals of Cariboo, of 1866

I n the song *Dancing Gals of Cariboo* James Anderson takes the voice of the Hurdy dancers. *The German Lasses* presumably gives Anderson's views of these women, whereas in this song he tries to show, in a rather comic voice, how the Hurdies feel. There is little doubt that many miners "cast sheep eye's" at the Hurdies. Clearly some fell in love and some more in lust, as evident from the Hurdies who stayed on in Cariboo to marry. It is also clear that at $1.00 a dance plus the cost of drinks, of which the Hurdies got a cut, it was not hard for a young in-lust miner to "spend his all" on the Hurdies.

The "four and twenty Welshmen, all sitting in a row," refers to the Company of Welsh Adventurers, a group of 24 miners who arrived in 1863, led by Captain John Evans and supported by British capital. They mined for two years with expenses of $26,000 and only retrieved $450 in gold. Men deserted regularly, and when the enterprise failed in 1864 all but Evans and few others scattered. For a time, however, they were the centre of a large Welsh community that was responsible for building the Cambrian Hall in Barkerville.

Hurdy Gurdy Dancers in Barkerville, 1865

"Hurdy Gurdy Damsels"

There are three descriptions of the above named "ladies" here, they are unsophisticated maidens of Dutch extraction, from "poor but honest parents," and, morally speaking, they really are not what they are generally put down for. They are generally brought to America by some speculating, conscienceless scoundrel of a being commonly called a "Boss Hurdy." This man binds them to his service until he has received about a thousand per cent for his outlay. The girls receive a few lessons in the terpsichorean art, are put into a kind of uniform, generally consisting of a red waist cotton print skirt, and a half mourning head-dress resembling somewhat in shape the topknot of a male turkey, this uniform gives them a grotesque appearance. Few of them speak English, but they soon pick up a few popular vulgarisms, and like so many parrots they use them indiscriminately on all occasions; if you bid one of them good morning, your answer will likely be "itsh sphlaid out" or "you bet your life."

The hurdy style of dancing differs from all other schools. If you ever saw a ring of bells in motion you have seen the exact positions these young ladies are put through during the dance, the more muscular the partner, the nearer the approximation of the ladies' pedal extremities to the ceiling, and the gent who can hoist his "gal" the highest is considered the best dancer; the poor girls as a general thing earn their money very hardly."

Cariboo Sentinel, September 6, 1866

"Departures," *Cariboo Sentinel* September 13, 1866

The gayer portion of our community were doomed to deplore with sad regret the departure on Monday last of two of the fair terpischorian artistes, who were wont to "trip the light fantastic" in Martin's saloon for months past, and whose benignant smiles softened the hearts and lightened the pockets of many a susceptible youth. Whether from the deep interest felt for the departing damsels, or from curiosity or some other unexplained cause, true it is and of verity, that an unusual number of our citizens were congregated around Barnard's stage when it left Richfield, and if the tears that fell thick and fast from the eyes of one of the disconsolate fair ones were any criterion of her feelings of affection for any one member of that crowd, the fortunate individual ought to have taken compassion on the poor girl's grief.

Ashcroft Saloon

The Dancing Gals of Cariboo, of 1866

Air — "Young Man from the Countree"

We are dancing girls in Cariboo,
And we're liked by all the men,
In gum boots and a blanket coat—
And e'en the upper ten!
We all of us have swee-eet-hearts,
But the dearest of all to me!
Is that young man who wistfully
Casts those sheep's-eyes at me!
       Chorus—"Is that young man," etc.

O ev'ry night at eight o'clock,
We enter the saloon—
Altho' it may be vacant then,
'Tis crowded very soon.
Then all the boys they stare at us,
But we do not mind that so
Like those four-and-twenty Welshmen,
All sitting in a row.
       Chorus—"Like those," etc.

O' what a charming thing it is,
To have a pretty face—
To know that one can kill as well
In calico as lace;
We steal the hearts of everyone,
But the dearest of all to me,
Is that dear boy with the curly head,
Who loves me faithfully,
       Chorus—"Is that dear boy," etc.

To all the boys of Cariboo,
This moral—which is right—
From the dancing gals of Cariboo,
You may see on any night—
"Before we either give our hearts,
Or yet our sympath-ee,
You must be like this dear young man,
Who spends his all on me!"
       Chorus—"You must be," etc.

Sawney's Letters and Cariboo Rhymes by James Anderson

Words: James Anderson
Tune: A variant of *Young Man of the Countree*; also known as *Paddy West* or *Tramps and Hawkers.*
Arrangement: Cathryn Wellner
Vocals: Cathryn Wellner, Caridwen Irvine, Michele Law

Hurdy Fiddlers
This class of musician (pardon the misnomer) have also a school of their own, in which melody and euphony have no part. Noise is the grand object. The one who can make the most noise on the fiddle, and shout his calls the loudest, is amongst the hurdy artists considered the most talented. Sometimes, to increase the power of the orchestra (which seldom consists of more than two violins— more properly Fiddlers in this case), they sing and play, and in passing up Broadway, Barkerville, in the evening, you may hear them letting off steam as if their lungs were made of cast iron, and the notes forged with a sledge hammer.
    Cariboo Sentinel,
    September 1866

Kelly piano,
Kelly Hotel,
Barkerville

The Seller of Souls
The way they dance in this country

Dancing was not confined to saloons, dance halls and ballrooms. Homes saw dances as did forts of the HBC, old "Here Before Christ." Overlanders mentioned dances at posts they passed and when 17-year-old Fred Nagle came up the Cariboo Trail in 1864 he described a dance at Fort Alexandria.

> "The dance took place last night. There were all the men from the boats [HBC bateaux from north arrived on 1st] and the men that are employed about the Fort and Farms. The ladies consisted of the (maidens of the forest) some of them wives of the men. Mr. Ogden played the fiddle, and 2 of the men also took turns in playing. The drum was a tin can and one of the indians was the drummer." Saturday, Sept. 3rd

Fred went to bed early and complained that the festivities kept him awake until the party broke up at 1:30 a.m.

> *Going Down – The fall migration has regularly set in. Each trip of Barnard's stages takes away a number of our most prominent citizens, who go down to spend the winter in Victoria… Amongst the passengers we noticed with regret Master Frank Wriggleshuth, who leaves behind no one more skilled in the art of violin playing; and through the long and dreary winter nights just before us his presence will be very much missed by those who have so often tripped the "light fantastic" to the sweet music so often discoursed by his masterly hand.*
> Cariboo Sentinel, October 2, 1868

The Seller of Souls (Medley)

The way they dance in this country (narration)

Maun, Sawney, ye wad like to see
The way they dance in this kintre
They lift the lassies aff their feet
In sic a way that's no discreet—
That a' at since they let them drap.
Syne ilka lad begins to clap
An thro' the din, an' fun, an' stoure
Ye'll hear a voice say, "sock it to her!"
They whirl them round in waltz and galop
Wi' a real Glengarry walop;
They strike their hands, and beat their feet,
Then turn aboot, and syne they'll meet;
An' after such a dance, just think,
They walk up to the bar and drink!
They'll jingle glasses left an' right,
The dollar gane—then "Gesund act."

This is Sunday night and on the opposite side of the street then are no less than three Hurdy Gurdy or dancing houses in full blast—two of them are occupied by German dancing girls— four in each—and the third by Squaws. Just now the "Silver Lakes Varsovianna" is ringing in my ears and noise and music is carried on every night till four and sometimes six in the morning. If I am at all out of sorts I find it quite impossible to sleep—The "King of the Cannibal Islands" has just struck up—fancy such a place.... It has been raining dreadfully all day—there goes Lucy Long,—and I like it better than the hot days. I board now at the French Hotel at Richfield and walk up and down about half a mile twice and sometimes three times a day—the "Sultan Polka" and the "Edinburgh Quadrille" at the same time from the White Hurdies—and often stay up there all day.
    Robert Burrell to Miss McKenzie,
    Craigflower Farm, 22 July 1866

The Way they Dance in this Country
From James Anderson's Sawney's Letters, March 1866
Narration: Duncan Bell

The Seller of Souls —Instrumental medley
Hurdy dancing tunes, here named for the "boss-hurdy."
Traditional, public domain
St. Anne's reel; Lucy Long; Yankee Doodle-Annexation; Dan Tucker
Ken Hamm, guitar; Richard Wright, vocals; Caridwen Irvine, fiddle; Donna Konsorado, banjo; John Law, harmony vocals, mandolin; Michele Law, harmony vocals, bass; Jerry Paquette, harmony vocals; Cathryn Wellner, harmony vocals

Kellyville on Grouse Creek, 1868

The Lover's Lament

Chips, Christian Hagerman, author of *Lover's Lament*, born in Germany, 1825, was, like many gold rush people, known to most folks only by his nickname, Chips. Barkerville native Lottie Bowron says, "I didn't know his last name until he got married."

The Annie he writes to could be any one of several Annies who were in Barkerville at that time, from prostitute Annie Jones, who shortly would go to jail for prostitution, to brothel madam Annie Miller or even Annie Lindsay, soon to be Skinner, sister of Constable Lindsay. Whoever she was, Chips did not marry her. In 1882 he married Marie Mockel, a German woman who died a few years later.

The British Columbia goldfields are not a place one might expect a love song to be written but Chips's Lover's Lament is a poignant reminder to us that life 150 years ago in a rough, hard, cold mining camp was not that much different than it is today. Miners worked hard but still had time and the inclination to fall in love, suffer heartbreak, long for home and look forward to a better, easier life.

⟶⟋⟍⟍⟵

This song is a good example of what is usually called the "folk process," the method which moves a song from sheet music into that general group of songs called folk music. A close reading of the sheet music published by G. B. Demarest in New York in 1858 shows *Kitty Wells*, written by Charles E. Atherton, to be another of the

Plantation genre, sometimes called "dese, dem and dose" songs for imitating the supposed southern black idiom. Undated song sheets printed during the 19th century give the author as Thomas Sloan Jr. of Newark, N.J.

Kitty Wells was composed just in time to get caught up in the Civil War. Bobby Horton, in his monumental collection/recordings of Civil War songs, quotes a Confederate Army artillery soldier stationed at Fort Fisher in 1865. Johnny House said *Katy Wells* was the privates' favorite song— especially when played on the banjo. Already the name had changed slightly. The tune that Horton records, however, is similar to, but not the same as, Atherton's sheet music. It has been "rounded out" with simplified phrasing and a modified musical range and changed from 4/4 time to 2/4. It is Horton's version we have recorded.

Horton's version has also dropped the offensive words "darkey" found on both sheet music and song sheets. Another version sung in the 21st century has truncated the verses, making them four lines rather than eight, and changed darkey to brothers.

The song was popular enough that it reached Barkerville, as *Kitty Wells*. Perhaps a traveling music troupe brought it to town or another miner got a song sheet in the mail from the U.S. Also, sheet music and song sheets traveled nearly as fast and served a similar purpose as today's recordings. Chips obviously knew the original words, as he left them in quotes in this song. The first two lines of the original, for instance, are:

"You ask what makes this darkie weep,

Why he like others am not gay…"

Chips put his own experience to the tune and sent it off to the local paper, the readers of which may well have known who this Annie was.

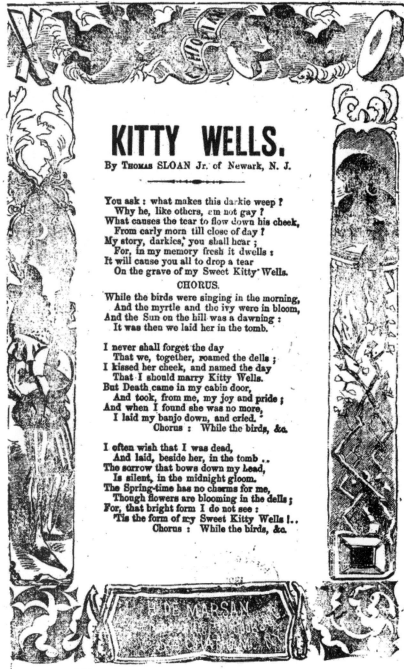

KITTY WELLS.

By Thomas SLOAN Jr. of Newark, N. J.

You ask : what makes this darkie weep ?
  Why he, like others, am not gay ?
What causes the tear to flow down his cheek,
  From early morn till close of day ?
My story, darkies, you shall hear ;
  For, in my memory fresh it dwells :
It will cause you all to drop a tear
  On the grave of my Sweet Kitty Wells.

CHORUS.

While the birds were singing in the morning,
  And the myrtle and the ivy were in bloom,
And the Sun on the hill was a dawning :
  It was then we laid her in the tomb.

I never shall forget the day
  That we, together, roamed the dells ;
I kissed her cheek, and named the day
  That I should marry Kitty Wells.
But Death came in my cabin door,
  And took, from me, my joy and pride ;
And when I found she was no more,
  I laid my banjo down, and cried.
      Chorus : While the birds, &c.

I often wish that I was dead,
  And laid, beside her, in the tomb ..
The sorrow that bows down my head,
  Is silent, in the midnight gloom.
The Spring-time has no charms for me,
  Though flowers are blooming in the dells ;
For, that bright form I do not see :
  'Tis the form of my Sweet Kitty Wells !..
      Chorus : While the birds, &c.

H. DE MARSAN

732

The Lover's Lament

AIR - "KITTY WELLS"

I "asked" what made my Annie "weep,"
Why she, "like others, was not gay?"
What secret sorrow weighed so deep?
To chase her happy smile away.
The cause, my comrades, I did "hear,"
From her sweet lips that very day;
Then she fondly whispered in my ear,
Wilt thou be true, my love, oh! say.

CHORUS.
 "While the birds were singing in the
    morning,"
In joyous welcome of the day—
When "the sun" each rose was adorning,
"It was then" she whispered—love, oh! say.

 "I never shall forget the" spot,
Where "we together" met that day;
In accents changed she asked me not,
Such very silly things to say.
So now this dream of love is o'er,
And she is happy, blythe and gay;
She never breathes those words of yore,
Wilt thou be true, my love, oh! say.

The Lover's Lament by Chips, Barkerville, *Cariboo Sentinel*, February 27, 1869
Tune: Kitty Wells— Charles E. Atherton or Thomas Sloan Jr.; public domain
Arrangement: Richard Wright and Cathryn Wellner
Richard Wright, vocals, autoharp; Ken Hamm, guitar; Caridwen Irvine, fiddle; Donna Konsorado, banjo; John Law, harmony vocals, mandolin; Michele Law, harmony vocals, bass; Cathryn Wellner, harmony vocals

W.G.R. Hind

The Old Red Shirt
Blacks in Cariboo

R ebecca Gibbs, author of *The Old Red Shirt*, was a black washerwoman in Barkerville, the only woman poet published in the *Cariboo Sentinel* and part of a significant black or, as the census of the day recorded, "African" community.

Minorities were the norm during gold rush days. Everyone was part of a minority. Men and women came from literally around the world. There were as many accents in Barkerville as there were shovels. Women, no matter their nationality, were a minority in numbers. The only race that was not a minority was the Chinese. At times they were fully half the population.

Blacks, however, were a minority and visible. Africans, the official records called them. "Coloured" was carved in gravemarkers, lest we forget. There were many scattered along the creeks, perhaps hundreds. Some were former slaves like Dan Williams. There were British businessmen like Wellington Delaney Moses and his neighbour David Lewis who had a bath house. Dr. Jones the Dentist from Salt Spring Island was black, as was J. Lawrence the Horsefly miner who wrote Skedaddler and other songs, and miners like the men of the Davis company.

In 1865 author Matthew Macfie wrote: "The descendants of the African race resident in the colonies are entitled to some notice. About 300 of them inhabit Victoria, and upwards of 100 are scattered throughout the farming settlements of the island and British Columbia. The chief part came to the country some time previous to the immigration of 1858, driven from California by social taboo and civil disabilities. They invested the sums they brought with them in land…"

The black immigration to B.C. was, as Macfie indicated, a result of increased pressure on minorities in California, including a move to prohibit "Negro" immigration. A delegation met with Governor James Douglas in Victoria, and soon 300 to 400 black families moved to the colony. Some of those headed for the Cariboo goldfields. Wellington Delaney Moses, a member of the Pioneer Committee that negotiated with Douglas, is perhaps the best known.

Three blacks who took up land were John K. Giscombe, Henry McDame and John L. McLean, who preempted land on the west side of the Fraser near Quesnellemouth in September 1862. The creek was then known as Henry's Creek or Nigger Creek. It later became Bouchie Creek. McLean is buried in the Camerontown Cemetery. His headboard reads "J.L.B. McLean (coloured)."

South of Quesnel a black roadhouse keeper had a place at Alexandria. Another, Bill Smith, had the "Nigger's" place at the head of Lightning Creek and over toward Antler was another by the same name. In Barkerville a significant black community existed. It included Dr. William Jones, Barkerville dentist, and his brother Elias. They were educated at Oberline College in Ohio. Their father had purchased his freedom from North Carolina, and the family moved to Salt Spring Island in the Gulf Islands near Victoria. Another brother, John Jones, taught school on Salt Spring where many black emigrants had settled.

Other Cariboo blacks included I. P. Gibbs, a barber who worked with Wellington Moses for a time. He was likely related to poet Rebecca Gibbs. John Anderson was a correspondent for a San Francisco newspaper. Harris Greenbury was a charcoal burner after whom Mount Greenbury near Wells is named. Mrs. Ann Wheeler lived in Richfield. Aaron Skank worked on the Dutch Bill hydraulic claim and broke a leg in a mining accident. Henry "Nigger" Steele kept a restaurant. Miss Hickman kept a lunch house. Isaac Dickson or Dixie, had a "Shampooing Establishment" and contributed to the *Cariboo Sentinel* in what might be called a black southern dialect. He once got into a knife fight with a Spaniard by the name of Rosario. There were miners such as Charles Gray, William Port, Henry Knight and Henry Allen, who hanged himself in his cabin in April 1868.

On the surface, at least, there appears to have been little racial prejudice against blacks, though doubtless some of the Southern boys in town did not appreciate their free presence. In his diaries Moses does not mention racial tensions beyond the normal arguments of any mining community.

As seen in the songs and poems of J. Lawrence (see *Skedaddler*), however, blacks in Cariboo lost no love on the racial tendencies of the Southern States.

Like the Cornish miners, the Masons and the Canadians, the blacks of Barkerville took strength in their ties with those of similar background. In doing so they contributed to the mosaic of the goldfields and the development of Barkerville.

James Anderson, the Scots Bard of Cariboo has gone down in the history of Williams Creek as the poet laureate of miners. But while his folk poetry left us with a valuable image of miners' life, he was by no means the only poet of Cariboo. The Bard of Lowhee, an anonymous contributor to the *Cariboo Sentinel* was another poet, as was John Fraser, the son of Simon Fraser, who committed suicide on the creeks.

One of most prolific creek poets, however, was Mrs. Rebecca Gibbs, a black laundress. Gibbs was born in Philadelphia in 1808 and judging from her literary works was well educated. She seems to have moved to California for the gold rush of '49, as she arrived in Victoria in 1858 with other black immigrants from California. Rebecca, according to her obituary in the San Francisco *Elevator* of December 20, 1873, was the "wife of Richard Gibbs," who died in 1864. His death left her alone at age 56 and likely precipitated her move to Barkerville, perhaps at the suggestion of I. P. Gibbs or Moses. So Rebecca started over at age 56. There was always work in the goldfields for women who could dance, bake or wash.

Her poems, however, seem to indicate she was on Williams Creek by 1862. In this case Rebecca was one of half a dozen women who wintered on the creeks during 1862/63, perhaps the woman R. Byron Johnson refers to in his *Very Far West* as "old Nigger Mary (a fat negress who did washing for the miners)." Certainly she was here by 1865, when she took out a mining license.

Barkerville, 1868, before the fire (R. Maynard)

Gibbs was likely related to Barkerville barber I. P. Gibbs and his brother Mifflin Gibbs, a prominent black who had a newspaper in San Francisco, moved to Victoria and then became a lawyer in the U.S. They both came to B.C. with their mother Marin Gibbs who by some reports spent time in Barkerville. All were from Philadelphia.

Gibbs's first poem in the *Cariboo Sentinel* was written in August 1868 to celebrate Canada's first Dominion Day.

"Canada, now a nation, stands alone,
In wealth and progress to full stature grown;
By nature's dictates we thitherward incline,
British Columbia must with her combine."

There was little doubt that Rebecca Gibbs was a Dominionist when she closed with the line, "Shall hail with triumph each Dominion Day."

Gibbs was operating a laundry by the summer of 1868, for at that time she wrote her classic poem *The Old Red Shirt*, published September 9, 1868, in the *Cariboo Sentinel*. Gibbs asks merchants to have pity on the men who work the mines and bring them their money. The color of the shirt is significant. Although color photography was not common in the 1860s, paintings and written descriptions often show or mention the red and blue shirts that made up a miner's uniform. They were the colors of the day.

Gibbs closes with a verse reflecting the loss of home life felt by most people on the creeks.

> "Far from these mountains a poor mother mourns
> The darling that hung by her skirt,
> When contentment and plenty surrounded the home
> Of the miner that brought me the shirt."

Gibbs's laundry burned down in the fire of September 1868. It was reported in the *Elevator*, a newspaper for blacks in San Francisco, that she had lost her building but saved everything else. After the fire she was one of the first to rebuild. Within ten days, at age 60, she had a new shop next to the Cariboo Sentinel. Of the fire she wrote:

> "Come ye many sufferers, and testify with me,
> How this village flourished, in the year of '63;
> Although it did lack nothing in the year of '64.
> It then sustained a thousand, aye a thousand men or more.
> Still years roll on until, it reaches sixty-eight,
> And we are still together, and with you I share my fate;
> We hear distressed mothers, and children in the street—
> Inhabitants of Cariboo, why should we then not weep.
>
> "The Almighty architect, though wicked we have been,
> Looked down and smiled upon us, when we commenced
> again;
> We viewed this waste laid village, with all her wealth and
> pride
> As Sodom and Gomorrah, this cannot be denied..."

A few months later Gibbs wrote a poem lauding *The Gallant Fire Brigade*. In April, with spring in the air but snow still deep on the ground, she wrote of a robin that came to her door but wouldn't stay, needing the freedom of the air. That summer mining accidents prompted a short verse, *On the recent Accidents*.

In June 1869 she wrote a poem that editor Robert Holloway considered too personal or libelous to print, verses that evidently criticized some leading citizen. She retaliated with a lengthy piece headed with, "Applicable to many cases in general, and none in particular: Consolatory to whom it may concern."

The piece criticized the community for being taken in by a claim owner, unidentified, who ran up bills all over town and then took "leg bail" and "skedaddled" out of town. She wrote it in an unusual meter for her, one similar to Alfred Tennyson's *The Charge of the Light Brigade*, written in 1864.

"Yet another unfortunate,
Weary of debt,
Has with 'leg bail' importunate
Creditors met."

A poem/song on the same theme as was written by black miner J. Lawrence in the following song, *Skedaddler*. Gibbs's poem was penned at Lightning Creek, June 1869, indicating she had moved west a few miles, but later poems were again signed Barkerville.

Poems followed on a vision of an angel she saw and later a plea for something better than hoping for wealth from a river. In June 1870 there was a poem *On the Death Of Judge Brew*, Chartres Brew, the former Chief Commissioner of Police for B.C. and then Gold Commissioner and County Court Judge at Richfield. This is the last recorded poem of Rebecca Gibbs and likely her last season in Barkerville. The rent on her crown lots in Barkerville was paid until April 25, 1870. In an 1871 directory she was still operating a laundry in Barkerville but soon moved to Victoria where she took up work as a nurse.

[ORIGINAL.]

ON THE RECENT ACCIDENTS.

Time is flying, time is flying,
Like water down the swiftest stream ;
Men are dying—this is trying—
Whilst the blood flows through their veins.
Who can tell the fatal hour
When man's strong mind and all his power
Shall fade away as the withered leaf
Of the sturdy oak, in the forest bleak.
Though man is doomed to sleep away
Beneath the clods of earthly clay,
His soul may soar to thrones above,
And there be spent in peace and love.

REBECCA GIBBS.

On November 14, 1873, Rebecca died of bronchitis, according to her death record. "She died in my house on Johnson Street," reported barber Randall Caesar. Her obituary was just a few lines in the *British Colonist*. A longer obituary in the *Elevator* indicating she had been caring for a man with brain fever, "erysiphilas" [erysipelas], who had been leeched and bled freely. It was surmised that Rebecca had an open cut and had been infected. She became ill and died in 10 days. She is buried in Victoria's Ross Bay Cemetery, Plot A71E30. No one wrote a poem for this poet of Cariboo.

The Old Red Shirt (narration)

A miner came to my cabin door,
>His clothes they were covered with dirt;
He held out a piece he desired me to wash,
>Which I found was an old red shirt.

His cheeks were thin and furrowed,
>His eyes they were sunk in his head;
He said he had just got work.
>And would be able to earn his bread.

He said that the garment was torn,
>And asked me to give it a stitch,
But found it was thoroughly worn,
>Which proved he was not very rich.

O! miners with good paying claims,
>O! traders who wish to do good,
Have pity on men who earn your wealth,
>And grudge not the poor miner his food.

Far from these mountains a poor mother mourns
>The darling that hung by her skirt,
When contentment and plenty surrounded the home
>of the miner that brought me the shirt.

Barkerville, Sept. 3, 1868.

Rebecca Gibbs, *Cariboo Sentinel*, September 9, 1868
Narration: Cathryn Wellner

Horsefly 1865.

"The Skedaddler—

I'm dead broke - I'm dead broke - So I've nothing to loose,
I've the wide world before me to live, where I choose.—
I'm at home in the wild woods, Wherever I be —
I'm dead broke, I'm dead broke - The Skedaddler is free —

The Creditors curse me - I care not a straw —
I heed not old Beytie - I laugh at his law —
There is game in the mountains, the rivers yield fish
And for Gold - I can prospect - Wherever I wish —

The Skedaddler

J. Lawrence did not indicate a tune for this song when he wrote of those who "skedaddled" from Cariboo, leaving debts and responsibilities behind. Homer, in his Odyssey, uses the word skedasis to describe a "scattering or dispersing." The term became popular during the U.S. Civil War and prompted George Danskin to write a song titled "Skedaddle" in 1862. It bears no resemblance to this song by Lawrence.

Black miner Lawrence was familiar with the term from the U.S., which it appears he left to escape racial problems. In other poetry he hopes the Southern states will lose and he will be able to go back:

"Then by Golly—won't we cheek,
Our former fizzled masters.
Oh then I'll travel through the South,
And in spite of Every Noodle
I'll clap my fingers to my nose—
And whistle —Yankee Doodle."

Though company-operated mines were still doing well in 1865, there were many men who could not find a paying claim or even a paying job. They skedaddled for the coast or homes, sometimes finding work with the road crews that were pushing the Cariboo Road into the mines.

Horsefly refers to the Horsefly River, on the south slope of the Cariboo Mountains, actually the first gold strike in Cariboo. The town centered around those claims was known as Harper's Camp, now Horsefly village.

68

Quod, is an old term for jail, or the compound prisoners exercised in. Begbie is, of course, Judge Matthew Baillie Begbie, known for his strict upholding of British law.

Jaw, is jawbone, or credit, referring to the "gift of the gab" some used to try and gain credit. One Cariboo establishment had a horse jawbone hung on the wall with the sign, "None of this here."

The Skedaddler

I'm dead broke - I'm dead broke - so I've nothing to loose [sic] -
I've the wide world before me to live, where I choose -
I'm at home in the wild woods, wherever I be -
'Tho dead broke, 'tho dead broke, the Skedaddler is free.

'Tho Creditors curse me - I care not a straw -
I heed not old Begbie - I laugh at his law -
There is game in the Mountains, the rivers yield fish,
And for Gold - I can prospect wherever I wish.

Where I fancy a spot; I my blankets unfold -
And remain for a time there - to prospect for gold -
And ne'er as a debtor - shall I go to Quod -
While my keep I can make - with my Gun, and my rod.

While I sit by my fire; and my baccy - I blow -
I heed not the cold winds, the frost or the snow -
'Tho alone in the Mountains, at least I am free -
'Tho the Ground is by [sic] bed and my roof - a pine tree -

When I think on the past, I can't see I'm in fault.
'Tho I worked like a horse - Yet I ne'er made my salt.
When my prospects were blighted, they stopped all my Jaw -
And 'tho honest at heart; I'm nowhere an outlaw.

Yet 'tho cleaned out and fizzled - I do not despair -
There's a land far from this one - I soon shall be there -
And if Providence leaves me, my hands and my health
The Skedaddler may yet win both honour and wealth.

    J. Lawrence, Horsefly 1865 (BCARS)

Tune: A variant of Rye Whiskey, Public domain, as taken from the
   singing of Phil Thomas.
Arrangement: Richard Wright.
Richard Wright, vocals; Ken Hamm, vocals, guitar; Caridwen Irvine,
   fiddle; John Law, vocals, mandolin; Michele Law, bass

Barkerville fire, 1868

Hard Times
Come Again No More

Hard on the heels of the miners in any gold rush were the missionaries, the priests and parsons, but though they had their adherents and followers they were for the most part ministers to a small flock in a cold, hard land. Snow was deep, winters eight months long, the creeks cold and gravel heavy and hard.

Speaking of a winter just past Rev. Reynard of St. Savior's wrote:

We were poor, my lord, and the cold made life all the harder. We were camped at nights round the fire in the most sheltered part of the house, the little ones crying from the cold ....

A bottle of port wine froze under my wife's pillow the day the baby was born, although the bedstead touched the stove in which the fire was maintained...

Hoarfrost covered the windows half an inch thick; nailheads were like English daisies; the boards cracked like pistol shots, and the knots flew out with great noise.

If the decrease of income be not made up my wife and children will have to leave before next winter. I cannot allow them to face another such time of hardship.

Reverend Reynard, Williams Creek, Winter 1868

If there is one Stephen Foster song appropriate for Williams Creek, Wild Horse Creek or Rock Creek, it must be *Hard Times*. While a few miners and investors went home wealthy, the majority of gold rushers saw little but hard times. The mines were further away than most travelers imagined, the country rougher. Trails were rough, bridges often non-existent, biting insects vicious enough to drive men to walk all night trying to escape the whining and blood sucking. Money disappeared quickly at the roadhouses, which charged what miners thought were enormous sums for simple meals. When they reached the gold creeks, in tatters and broke, the gold was not lying in the creek beds waiting for them as so many expected.

When John Clapperton's party reached Antler Creek in early 1862, they quickly summarized what was needed to find gold:

"We prospected round, with no better success than yesterday, feeling thoroughly convinced that to undo the bolts and bars of nature's treasure vaults was a work of time, requiring a deal of capital, experience and indomitable perseverance. The hundreds we met with every day, who had been longer in the country than we, looking woe-begone and dispirited, confirmed our own notion that there was no gold to be found near the surface."

Clapperton had hit the nail on the head. The men who found gold were invariably part of a company and with few exceptions had capital, previous experience in California or the lower Fraser, and determination. John Cameron, Billy Barker, James Loring, I. P. Diller, Dick Willoughby—the list of successful miners showed years of digging, a successful strike or money from home for capital and perseverance. Men who had walked from the coast were soon out of provisions and just as soon out of money, as prices were high. As they ran out of food and dollars they looked around for a friend who was well fixed.

Clapperton again: "We tried to get work from some of the claims that were paying well, but all of them were full-handed and had lots of friends, just in the same fix as ourselves, to whom work would be given in preference to strangers."

Clapperton and his men were relying on selling their horse to provide escape money. It died on Bald Mountain. In July they packed up what goods they had and set out to escape, walking through days of rain. Like most miners they ran out of provisions, sold clothes and firearms, rustled a beef, went hungry and borrowed money until they reached Yale, where they found some work to pay expenses. These were hard times.

Those who stayed on the creeks prospecting, mining or working for wages seldom stayed all year. Most miners, whether claim partners or working miners, left the cold mountain creeks for the winter, but a winter sojourn at the coast did not necessarily mean an escape from hard times. Dobson Prest, one of the overlanders who walked west in the spring and summer of 1862 wrote home from Victoria on what he called a gloomy Christmas Day, 1863.

"I have been thrown together with a first-rate lot of fellows to live with this winter, 2 Irishmen, 2 Canadian, 2 Americans I Dutchman... The rain commenced one month earlier this winter than last, which has made it rather bad for those that returned from the mines strapped, as work is scarce and wages very low. There are very few men in this country make anything more than a living in the winter time...there are dozens of mechanics that can't get even labouring work to do. Men commenced to arrive from the mines long before harvesting was ended and it reduced wages to one dollar per day."

Dobson Prest, Hurricane Hall, December 25, 1863 (BCARS)

The glory of wealth and returning home to a hero's welcome eluded all but a few. Many died on the trails and creeks. Many returned home broke and defeated. A few stayed in British Columbia to open businesses, farms or ranches or found work and stayed. All would

Stephen Foster

have agreed with Foster's chorus, "Oh! Hard Times come again no more."

Stephen Collins Foster was born July 4, 1826, and died January 13, 1864, the son of William Barclay Foster and Elisa Clayland [Tomlinson] Foster, married in 1807. He had three sisters and four brothers. In 1850 he married Jane Denny McDowell.

Among Foster's most popular songs are: *Oh! Susanna* (1848), *De Camptown Races* (1850), *Old Folks at Home* [Swanee River] (1851), *My Old Kentucky Home, Good-*

Night! (1853), *Jeanie With the Light Brown Hair* (1854), *Gentle Annie* (1856), and *Beautiful Dreamer* (1862). Foster was perhaps the father of but certainly one of the main writers of the genre that became know as "minstrel and plantation songs," an immensely popular form during much of the 19th century.

Lines and phrases from his songs became part of the idiom of the day, used in other songs and in everyday conversation. Barkerville native resident Gentle Annie, for example, may well have been named as some kind of joke after Foster's song of that name.

In *Hard Times* we hear the echoes once again of the Black community of the Cariboo goldfields. Stephen's brother Morrison Foster wrote his biography and told the story of the song.

"When Stephen was a child, my father had a mulatto girl named Olivia Pise, the illegitimate daughter of a West Indian Frenchman, who taught dancing to the upper circles of Pittsburgh society early in the [19th] century. 'Lieve', as she was called, was a devout Christian and a member of a church of shouting colored people. The little boy was fond of their singing and boisterous devotions. She was permitted to often take Stephen to church with her… A number of strains heard there, and which, he said to me, were too good to be lost, have been preserved by him, short scraps of which are incorporated in two of his songs, 'Hard Times Come Again no More' and 'Oh, Boys, Carry me 'Long.'"

Stephen Foster died in 1864, but his songs were immensely popular for years after his death, on stage, in parlours and around campfires.

In this version Cathryn Wellner sticks closely to Foster's original sheet music, using the phrasing and phrases that Foster intended, often forgotten in more recent versions.

Rev. Reynard's letter (see page 70)
Narration: Edd Wright

Hard Times Come Again No More
Words and music, Stephen Foster, 1855; Firth, Pond & Company, NY
Arrangement: Cathryn Wellner
Cathryn Wellner, vocals; Willie P. Bennett, harmonica; Ken Hamm, guitar, vocals; John Law, Michele Law and Richard Wright, harmony vocals
Links to sheet music at http://grassrootsgroup.com/sheetmusic.htm

HARD TIMES
Come again no More.

Let us pause in life's pleasures, and count its many tears,
　　While we all sup sorrow with the poor;
There's a song that will linger forever in our ears—
　　Oh, hard times, come again no more.

　　'Tis the song, the sigh of the weary—
　　　　Hard times, hard times, come again no more!
　　Many days you've lingered around my cabin door,
　　　　Oh, hard times, come again no more.

Here's a pale, drooping maiden, who toils her life away,
　　With a worn heart whose better days are o'er;
Though her voice would be merry, 'tis sighing all the day,
　　Oh, hard times, come again no more!

　　'Tis the song, the sigh of the weary—
　　　　Hard times, hard times, come again no more!
　　Many days you've lingered around my cabin door,
　　　　Oh, hard times, come again no more.

'Tis a sigh that is wafted across the troubled wave;
　　'Tis a wail that is heard upon the shore;
'Tis a dirge that is murmured around the lonely grave;
　　Oh, hard times, come again no more.

　　'Tis the song, the sigh of the weary—
　　　　Hard times, hard times, come again no more!
　　Many days you've lingered around my cabin door,
　　　　Oh, hard times, come again no more.

A. W. Auner, Song Publisher, N. E. cor. Eleventh & Market, Philadelphia, Pa.

The Overlanders in camp, 1862

Yellow Rose of Texas

The Yellow Rose of Texas was Emily Morgan West. As the legend goes she was a former slave or indentured servant, a woman of "high yellow" color, captured by or mistress to Mexican General Santa Anna during the Texas Revolution in 1836. She is said to have kept Santa Anna dallying in his tent long enough that his leaderless army lost the Battle of San Jacinto on April 21, 1836. Historians point out that the Texians won only because Sam Houston was drunk and the Texians decided to attack while the Mexicans engaged in their noon siesta.

Whatever the battle strategy, the song was also popular in Canada. Canadian Overlander Robert B. McMicking copied the words of the song into his 1862 overland diary.

Near Fort Ellice, Manitoba, enroute to the Cariboo Goldfields, Summer 1862: After supper some fished, others went shooting, and the musicians entertained. Tom Jones was on concertina, George Baillie on violin, John Fannin on cornet and circled around were thirty others, "playing on different kinds of Brass instruments, claanetts, flutes, violin and a concertina and others would gather in a group Singing over a few favorite pieces of Vocal Music," like "Castles in the Air," ... or "The Yellow Rose of Texas," whiling "away the hour of evening until bed time as merrily and pleasant as though in some grand concert hall of the first fashion in an eastern city."

James Sellars journal, 1862, from *Overlanders* by Richard Wright.

The words and music were first published in 1854 by Firth and Pond Co., New York, "composed and arranged expressly for Charles H. Brown by J.K."

The word "darkey," common in 19th century music and written in the original version of this song, is now considered offensive. The word soldier is now the accepted version, not inappropriately considering the

Robert B. McMicking

song was likely written by a black soldier fighting for Texas.

The phrase "sing of Rosa Lee" may refer to the extremely popular song of the day, *Rosalie the Prairie Flower*.

Words and Music: "J.K." - public domain
Arrangement: Richard Wright
Richard Wright, vocals, autoharp; Willie P. Bennett, harmonica; Ken Hamm, guitar, harmony vocals; Caridwen Irvine, fiddle; Donna Konsorado, banjo; John Law, harmony vocals, mandolin; Michele Law, harmony vocals, bass; Cathryn Wellner, harmony vocals

Sheet music sources:
The Lester S. Levy Sheet Music Collection has versions with harmonies .
Links to sheet music at http://grassrootsgroup.com/sheetmusic.htm

678

THE YELLOW ROSE

OF

TEXAS.

The music for this ballad can be be obtained at the extensive Music Establishment of Firth, Pond & Co. 547 Broadway, N. Y.

There's a yellow Rose in Texas that I am going to see,
No other darkey knows her, no darkey only me;
She cried so when I left her, it like to broke my heart,
And if I ever find her wo never more will part.

CHORUS.

She's the sweetest rose of color this darkey ever knew,
Her eyes are bright as diamonds, they sparkle like the dew.
You may talk about your Dearest May, and sing of Rosa Lee,
But the yellow rose of Texas beats the belles of Tennessee.

Where the Rio Grande is flowing and the starry skies are bright,
She walks along the river in the quiet summer night;
She thinks if I remember, when we parted long ago,
I promised to come back again, and not to leave her so.
CHORUS.—She's the sweetest rose of color, &c.

Oh! now I'm going to find her, for my heart is full of wo,
And we'll sing the song together, that we sung so long ago,
We'll play the banjo gailey, and we'll sing the songs of yore,
And the yellow rose of Texas shall be mine for ever more.
CHORUS.—She's the sweetest rose of color, &c.

Johnson, Song Publisher, Stationer & Printer, No. 7 N. Tenth St., 3 doors above Market, Phila.

Cards, Circulars, Bill-Heads, Hand-Bills, Posters, Labels, Ball, Raffle, Excursion and Party Tickets, Programmes, Ladies' Invitations, Checks, &c., neatly Printed, with accuracy and despatch.

Union Letter and Note Papers and Envelopes. New Songs of all kinds for the Union, at Johnson's, No. 7 North Tenth St., Philadelphia.

Come Back Faro

I t has become a popular gold rush myth that Cariboo citizens were so honest and Judge Matthew Baillie Begbie's law so just and stern, that crime was almost non-existent. You could leave gold sitting on the boardwalk; prostitution was unheard of, and gambling something only the Chinese and those decadent Californians subscribed to. In truth, while the B.C. was not as rough and lawless as California during the gold rush of '49, neither was it the peaceful utopia so often painted. Murders were not uncommon; there were knife fights and shootings in the mining camps; drunkenness was commonplace, prostitution thrived, as did both white and Chinese brothels, and gambling was rampant. James Anderson, writing his first letter to Sawney in February 1864 said,

> "There's a set of men up here,
> Wha never works thro' a' the year,
> A kind o' serpents, crawlin' snakes,
> That fleece the miner o' his stakes;
> They're gamblers—honest men some say,
> Tho' its quite fair to cheat in play—
> If it's NO KENT O'—I ne'er met

An honest man a gambler yet!
O, were I Judge in Cariboo,
I'd see the laws were carried thro',
I'd hae the cairds o' every pack
Tied up into a gunny sack,
Wi' a' the gamblers chained thegither,
And banished from the creek forever."

Judge Begbie eventually banned the card game Faro. In this song Anderson writes as if to lament the passing of "a fine old man," the card game Faro, although his tongue is firmly planted in his cheek.

Anderson, in penning this song, indicated it was to the "Air—*Peter Gray*." In the 1800s there were many versions of Peter Gray, a song about a young man from Pennsylvania who goes west in search of furs and is scalped by "Indians." The song was found on dozens of broadsides and song sheets published in the U.S. during the mid-1800s. While the verses all used a similar tune the chorus varied, from *Blow Ye Winds of Morning* to the version used here which best suits Anderson's chorus. Peter Gray was sung in Barkerville's Theatre Royal in 1871 by Ephriam and the Cariboo Minstrels.

Paper collars were disposable collars, a nicety most miners had neither time nor money nor inclination to wear. Young Lansquenet refers to another card game, anything but young as it was introduced by German foot soldiers, soldiers of fortune, in the 15th century. It was often called lambs skinnet. Author Alexandre Dumas had the Three Musketeers playing the game in his novel.

White Pine, referred to in the last chorus, was an 1868 silver strike in Nevada.

Come Back Faro

I'll sing you a mournful song,
All of a fine old man,
Who liv'd some years in Cariboo,
All by his sleight of han'.

Chorus
Come back, Faro, come back, Faro, pray,
Or I'll sing tooral la de O!
Sing tooral la de A!

Altho' he lay in his bed all day,
He was wide awake at night;
And when the luck was on his side,
His face beamed with delight
        Chorus – Come back, Faro," etc.

I've often watched his little game,
And even been case-keeper;
And tho' his eyes were pretty sharp,
I've sometimes "snailed a sleeper."
        Chorus – "Come back Faro," etc

At times he'd grumble of hard luck,
And say he'd ne'er a dollar—
Yet he lived jolly as a lord,
And wore a paper collar.
        Chorus—"Come back Faro," etc.

Ah, many a time he found me grub,
When I had ne'er a red—
Now I must work ten hours a day,
Since good old Faro's dead.
        Chorus—"Come back Faro," etc.

But what is worse, I dare not dance,
Nor squeeze a little paw—
I'll tell the reason, but "don't ment'ch,"
I cannot "shoot my jaw."
        Chorus

Words: James
    Anderson
Music: "Peter Gray"
    - traditional,
    public domain
Arrangement:
    Richard Wright
Richard Wright,
    vocals, autoharp;
    Ken Hamm,
    guitar, harmony
    vocals; Cathryn
    Wellner,
    harmony vocals

GAMBLING CASE
James Loring, an old sport [gambler], brought a complaint before the Police Magistrate, on Monday last, charging two professional gentlemen in Barkerville, with having, on the evening of the 6th, in a room adjoining Parker & Sterling's saloon, kept a faro bank, dealt cards, and otherwise gambled, contrary to the statute 8 and 9 Vic. The accused appeared in court and having admitted the charge were each [fined] $242.50 with costs. The magistrate cautioned them to be more careful in future as there are people among them who were looking out for the moral good of the public.
    Cariboo Sentinel,
September 12, 1867

Some say old Faro was a rogue,
Tho' 'tis not my belief;
But if he were—then I am sure
Young Lansquenet's a thief,
　　　Chorus

Whate'er you were, old Faro, dear,
I'll not defame the dead—
Your ghost might haunt me some cold night,
And "freeze me out" in bed.

Last chorus:
Goodbye, Faro, goldbye, old Faro, dear,
And may you strike it in White Pine,
And may we strike it here.

Miner's Commandment Number 3
Thou shalt not go prospecting before thy claim gives out. Neither shalt thou take thy money, nor thy gold dust, nor thy good name, to the gaming table in vain; for monte, twenty-one, roulette, faro, lansquenet and poker, will prove to thee that the more thou puttest down the less thou shalt take up; and when thou thinkest of thy wife and children, thou shalt not hold thyself guiltless—but insane.

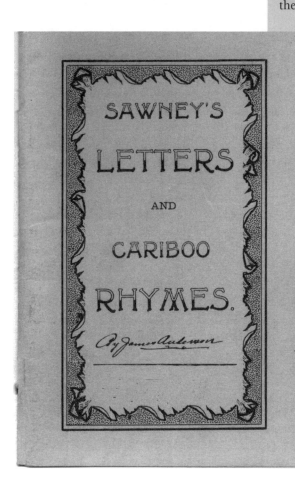

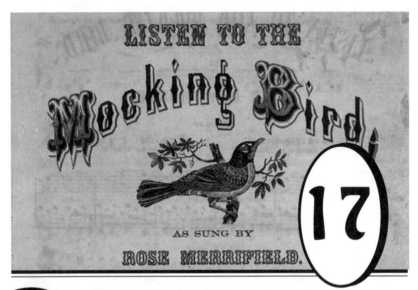

LISTEN TO THE

Mocking Bird

AS SUNG BY

ROSE MERRIFIELD.

17

The Cariboo Amateur Dramatic Association occupied their free time producing farces, plays, musicals, balls and entertainment evenings to keep themselves busy and the residents of the town entertained. According to the *Cariboo Sentinel* reviews, these productions were of a high standard.

Sometimes balls or benefits were held to raise funds for the hospital, the fire department, some miner or family in need, or even to send orphaned children to a children's home in Victoria. In one unfortunate case a woman who escorted two children and the town's monetary contribution to an orphanage in Victoria dumped the children and absconded, not only with the money but with one of Barkerville's sheriffs named Chisolm.

Travelling theatre troupes, sometimes called Minstrel troupes, were popular in the mining camps and towns of early British Columbia. Troupes such as Captain Jack Crawford, a Buffalo Bill cohort; the McGinty Family and the Potter Troupe made a circuit from Victoria, through New Westminster and Yale up to Barkerville to play in the saloons or the theatre. Some of the saloon owners such as P. Manetta and J. T. Scott, knew the travelling artists from when they had saloons in New Westminster. There Manetta ran the Eldorado Saloon and Scott the Pioneer Saloon and Theatre.

Another such group was Lafont and Ward's Troupe, with Stage Manager Tom Lafont, Business Manger Ned Ward and Musical Director Professor Wilson. Lafont's wife appeared on stage as did the two men and a Miss Montez and a Mr. Barry.

Theatre Royal, Barkerville.

LAFONT
AND
WARD'S
TROUPE
WILL APPEAR ON
Sunday Evening, July 26th,

In one of their chaste and Comical Entertainments.

STAGE MANAGER,	TOM LAFONT.
BUSINESS MANAGER,	NED WARD.
MUSICAL DIRECTOR,	PROFESSOR WILSON

PROGRAMME:

OVERTURE—Operatic,	BAND.
Opening Chorus,	Company.
Mocking Bird, with Imitations by Tom Lafont,	Mrs Lafont.
Nora's Beer Pullins,	Ned Ward.
Rock me to Sleep, Mother,	Mr Berry.
Annie Lisle,	Miss Montez.
Darling Mickey,	Tom Lafont

Anvil Chorus, by Ward, Lafont & Co.

WALK AROUND,
WHO'S DAT HEEL A BURNIN!

OVERTURE, - - ORCHESTRA.

CHINA ACT.

YUNG FU,	NED WARD
Mellean Man,	Mr Pearce

KATY AVOURNEEN,	MRS LAFONT

Comic Negro Dance, - - Tom Lafont.

JUANITA BALLAD,	MISS MONTEZ

Matrimonial Sweets—Duett,
BY MRS LAFONT AND MR WARD.

The whole to conclude with the laughable afterpiece entitled, the

MASQUERADE BALL,
Characters by the Company.

On Sunday evening, July 26th, they presented "one of their chaste and Comical Entertainments" in Barkerville's Theatre Royal. One of the songs Mrs. Lafont performed was "Mocking Bird, with imitations by Tom Lafont." We assume the imitations were sound imitations, rather than flights of fancy.

The orchestra was likely one made up from townsfolk. Their entertainment included the *Anvil Chorus*, an Overture, several songs, including *Katy Avourneen*, a parody of *Kathleen Mavourneen*, a popular sentimental piece usually sung by Irish tenors. Juanita covered the Latin side of their act and then there was a China Act and a Comic Negro Dance. For good measure they "concluded with the laughable afterpiece entitled the Masquerade Ball."

~ꝏꝿ~

Listen to the Mocking Bird was written by Alice Hawthorne, with sheet music published by Lee and Walker. It was respectfully dedicated to Aaron R. Duther, Esq. with the note that it was "as sung by Rose Merrifield." The song was a great hit, with various arrangements following close on its popularity. *Mocking Bird Echoes* was published, "a collection of beautiful variations, marches, waltzes, galops, quicksteps etc. upon this very popular melody." Later there was the "Grand Fantasia on the famous theme of "The Mocking Bird."

Septimus Winner

Alice Hawthorne was a pseudonym of Septimus Winner, born May 1827 in Philadelphia to Joseph E. Winner and Mary Ann Hawthorne. Winner was a composer, teacher, performer and music publisher. He also wrote under the names Mark Mason, Percy Guyer and Paul Stenton, but it was the genre of Hawthorne Ballads that drew most attention to him.

When Winner was 27 he owned a music store in Philadelphia and was acquainted with a young black boy, Dick Milburn (known as Whistling Dick), a street busker who collected coins for his whistling and guitar playing on the streets. His whistling sometimes turned to imitating a mockingbird. This attracted Winner and gave him the idea for a song. He published the work in April 1855 using the name Alice Hawthorne and credited Milburn with the melody. Milburn's name was dropped on subsequent printings, however, when Winner sold the rights to publishers Lee and Walker for $5. Whistling

Dick came out best—he got a job in Winner's store.

Within months the song hit all parts of North American and was soon popular all over Europe. Even King Edward VII of England later remembered whistling it as a child. For years afterward Southern mothers named their girls Hally or Hallie. By 1905 sheet music sales had reached approximately 20 million. The song has remained popular and is usually thought of as an old-timey tune of the 20th century, rather than having its origins in the mid 1800s. After 150 years it is still sung.

As a side note Winner found notoriety during this same period, 1862, when he was arrested for treason for writing and publishing "Give Us Back Our Old Commander: Little Mac, the People's Pride."

He wrote this song after Gen. Geo. McClellan was discharged as commander, Army of the Potomac, by Lincoln. The song sold 80,000 copies in two days. He was released only after destroying all remaining copies.

Winner wrote hundreds of songs and thousands of arrangements in his lifetime but is perhaps best remembered for two comic songs, *Ten Little Indians*, (one little, two little, three little...) and for *Der Deitcher's Dog*, better known as "Oh where, oh where ish mine little dog gone," also a great success.

NEW ADVERTISEMENTS.

CONCERT HALL
RICHFIELD

Mr. Victor Lange begs to inform the public that he has now opened a concert Hall at Richfield, opposite the "London and Paris Hotel." Mrs. Lange will preside at the Piano every evening, and will play some of the best Operas, the most popular Ballads, and every description of Dances.

None but the best brands of Liquors and Cigars served at the Bar.

July 6th, 1867, *Cariboo Sentinel*.

Listen to the Mockingbird

Words and music:
  Alice Hawthorne
  (Septimus Winner)
Arrangement:
  Cathryn Wellner
  and Richard
  Wright
Cathryn Wellner,
  vocals; Willie P.
  Bennett,
  harmonica; Ken
  Hamm, guitar,
  harmony vocals;
  Caridwen Irvine,
  fiddle; Donna
  Konsorado, banjo;
  John Law,
  mandolin,
  harmony vocals;
  Michele Law, bass,
  harmony vocals,
  Richard (Whistling
  Dick) Wright,
  whistling,
  autoharp

Sheet music sources:
The Lester S. Levy
  Sheet Music
  Collection has
  versions with
  harmonies.
Authors' collection -
  Piano arrangement
  for mixed voices:
Links to sheet music
  at http://
  grassrootsgroup.com/
  sheetmusic.htm

I'm dreaming now of Hally, sweet Hally, sweet
  Hally,
I'm dreaming now of Hally,
For the thought of her is one that never dies;
She's sleeping in the valley, the valley, the
  valley,
She's sleeping in the valley,
And the mocking bird is singing where she
  lies.

CHORUS
Listen to the mocking bird,
Listen to the mocking bird,
The mocking bird still singing o'er her grave;
Listen to the mocking bird,
Listen to the mocking bird,
Still singing where the weeping willows wave.

Ah! well I yet remember, remember, remember,
Ah! well I yet remember
When we gather'd in the cotton, side by side
'Twas in the mild September, September,
  September,
'Twas in the mild September,
And the mocking bird was singing far and
  wide.
CHORUS

When the charms of spring awaken, awaken,
  awaken,
When the charms of spring awaken,
And the mocking bird is singing on the bough,
I feel like one forsaken, forsaken, forsaken,
I feel like one forsaken,
Since my Hally is no longer with me now.
CHORUS

Harper's Weekly, December 23, 1871

Days of '49

Cattle were driven up from Oregon and Washington; goods came from California, miners, settlers and merchants—many came from south of the border. Americans had a profound effect on the development of B.C. during the early gold rush years, an influence that is still felt in B.C. today. There may have been British rule, but there certainly was American occupation.

The song *Days of '49* represents that California influence at the same time that it speaks to those miners who looked back on the days of '58 on the Fraser or '62 in the Cariboo. James Anderson, the Cariboo poet, later wrote a poem from Scotland with a similar reminiscent theme asking, "Oh, where are the boys of '63?"

The song comes from the oral tradition and to the best of our knowledge has not been credited to any particular author. Some versions have ten or twelve verses telling the stories of more diggers for gold.

We are the voices of the wandering wind,
Which moan for rest.
But rest can never find.
So! As the wind is, so is mortal life,
A Moan, a Sigh, A Sob, a Storm, a Strife –
    Williams Phillips' 1862 Overlander diary.

Narration: Ken Hamm

Days of '49

Oh here you see old Tom Moore,
A relic of former days.
They call me a bummer and a gin-sot too,
But what care I for praise?
For my heart is filled with the days of yore,
And oft I do repine,
For the days of old, the days of gold,
And the days of Forty-Nine.

Words and music:
    public domain
Arrangement: Richard
    Wright and Ken
    Hamm
Richard Wright,
    vocals; Ken Hamm,
    guitar

Chorus:
In the days of old, the days of gold,
How oft I do repine,
For the days of old, when we dug up the gold,
And the days of Forty-Nine.

I'd comrades then who loved me well,
A jolly, saucy crew;
There were some hard cases, I'll admit,
But they were brave and true;
Who'd never flinch, what're the pinch,
Would never fret or whine,
But like good old bricks, they stood the kicks,
In the days of Forty-Nine.

There was Kentuck Bill, I knew him well,
A fellow so full of tricks,
At a poker game he was always there,
And as heavy too, as bricks,
He'd play you a draw, he'd ante a slug,
And go a hatfull blind,
But in the game with Death, Bill lost his breath,
In the days of Forty-Nine.
Chorus

Days of '49

There was New York Jake, the butcher boy,
Who was always getting tight,
And whenever Jake went on a spree,
He was spoiling for a fight.
One day he ran agin' a knife,
In the hands of old Bob Cline,
So over Jake we held a wake,
In the days of Forty-Nine.
Chorus

There was Roarin' Bill from Buffalo.
I never will forget,
He'd roar all day and roar all night,
And I guess he's roaring yet.
He fell into a prospect hole,
Of a roarin' bad design,
And in that hole Jim roared out his soul,
In the days of Forty-Nine.
Chorus

Of all the comrades I have known
Not one remains to toast,
They have left me here in my misery,
Like some poor wandering ghost.
And as I pass from town to town,
Folks call me a travelling sign:
Saying: "Here's Tom Moore, a bummer sure,
From the days of Forty-Nine."

Fourth of July – The morning of the 4th was ushered in by our American friends with a salute of 34 guns in honor of the 34 States of the Union, which was again repeated at noon. Through the day the national ensigns of England and America floated over the principal buildings in town. With the exception of a little excitement caused by a few demonstrative individuals who took occasion to pay their respects rather too freely at the altar of the "jolly god" there was nothing occurred to mar the wonted good order of the community.
Cariboo Sentinel, July 8, 1867

FAREWELL!

Cold Cariboo, farewell!
I write it with a sad and heavy heart;
You've treated me so roughly that I feel,
'Tis hard to part.

'Twas all I asked of thee,
One handful of thy plenteous golden grain,
Had'st thou but yielded, I'd have sung "Farewell!"
And home again.

But, time on time, defeat!
Ah, cold and cruel, callous Cariboo!
Have eight years' honest persevering toil
No more of you?

Ah well, then since 'tis so—
Since Fate hath will'd I should no longer here—
I e'en submit, while disappointment starts
The hidden tear.

But still I'll picture thee
And some dear loved one in the days gone by,
And think what might have been, till dreaming brings
The soothing sigh.

Farewell! a fond farewell
To all thy friendships, kindly Cariboo!
No other land hath hearts more warm than thine,
Nor friends more true.
                              SAWNEY.
24th November, 1871.

Written by James Anderson
Narration: Duncan Bell

Days of '49 reprise

…They call me a bummer and a gin-sot too,
But what care I for praise?
For my heart is filled with the days of yore,
And oft I do repine,
For the days of old, the days of gold,
And the days of Forty-Nine.

Richard Wright, vocals; Ken Hamm, guitar

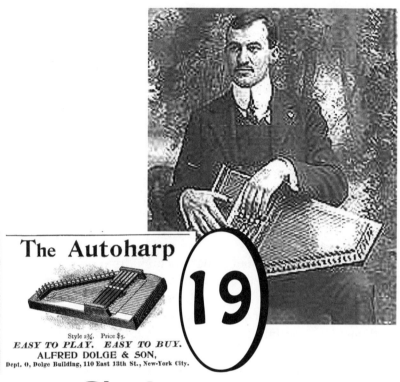

The Autoharp

Style 2¾. Price $5.
EASY TO PLAY. EASY TO BUY.
ALFRED DOLGE & SON,
Dept. O, Dolge Building, 110 East 13th St., New-York City.

The Instruments

The instruments used for the *Rough But Honest Miner* CD are for the most part period instruments.

Guitars were common in the 1800s although they were undergoing some changes. They were smaller than what we normally think of today and certainly not like the huge Martins so popular in the 1990s. Ken Hamm played an 1850s Bruno parlour guitar with a marvelous tone, one that fortunately blended particularly well with Richard's autoharps, more correctly called a chorded zither. Zithers were common in the 1800s, and the chorded versions were available by the early 1880s, perhaps as early as the late 1870s.

The pump organ or American organ played by Jack Velker on *The German Lasses* was an 1887 Bell pump organ, with "mouse-proof pedals." Jack explained that in earlier times mice had a taste for the carpets on the pedals, so mouse-proof was a great feature. The percussion heard in this track is not a boudrhan or step dancing, but Jack pumping like crazy on pedals that fed a leaky bellows. Jack

91

decided to make the problem an opportunity and added a percussion track by pumping in time with the tune.

Banjos and mandolins were popular instruments of the time as mentioned in diaries of the Overlanders. The mandolin was increasing in popularity while the banjo was already well established by the 1870s. The Civil War made many of these instruments common.

Harmonicas, a basic free-reed instrument similar in concept and origin to a harmonium or organ was, of course, popular then as it is now as a shirt-pocket instrument.

Fiddles were the required instrument for dances, whether played by Métis in HBC forts or by Hurdy fiddlers in the dance halls. No gold rush camp could be without several, and the players were highly prized as employees. For dances, whatever other instruments were available were added. Reverend Reynard introduced the fiddle into his church but not without some dissention from his congregation, who thought of the fiddle as only fit for playing the Devil's music.

Visiting a reconstructed gold rush town today shows only a shadow of what they once were. Not only were the streets crowded and rambunctious but the noise, the bustle, the music and dancing went on all night, not ceasing until the early hours of dawn. Miners worked hard and, if they could afford it, played hard.

Walk the silent streets of a Barkerville or Fort Steele or Quesnelle Forks some evening and listen well. Over the hollow sound of your footsteps on an empty boardwalk, you might hear the strains of *Lucy Long* or a Quadrille, a Galop or a Polka coming from the closed doors of a gold rush saloon. Some say they are still dancing.

"While I sit and write, the bones are sounding one side the fiddle on another, the banjo on another, the Cornopean and Saric horn peal forth their notes together with 12 or 14 of the best singers that I ever heard. The noise of all this together with the sight of so many of the pale-faced race, perfectly astonishes the redskins, as yet we have not been molested by them and we have passed through 2 nations viz. Chippawas and Crees and we are now on the margin of the Blackfeet."

Dobson Prest, in camp at Fort Edmonton, July 22nd, 1862, on overland journey to Cariboo.

Overlander camp from journal of W.H.R. Hind

About the Authors

This book and CD project is a combination of the interests and skills of writer/musician Richard Thomas Wright and storyteller/musician Cathryn Wellner. It combines their love of B.C. history and music with their skills as researchers.

Wright is well known as an historical writer and photographer, has explored much of this province and its history by canoe, on cross-country skis and by foot, and has spent many summers and a few winters in gold rush country. For several years Wright was an historical interpreter in Barkerville, creating the character of James Kelso.

He has had 22 books published, including *The Overlanders*, (recently republished) the story of the westward Canadian movement to the gold fields of British Columbia and *In a Strange Land*, a pictorial history of the Chinese in Canada. He has written over 500 magazine articles and is an award-winning columnist

Wright worked as a journalist for several years, first with the *Quesnel Cariboo Observer*, as managing editor of the *Cowichan News Leader* in Duncan, B.C., and as a locum editor for Cariboo Press.

Richard was the recipient of a B.C. Heritage Trust Award of Recognition in 1996, for "an outstanding commitment to the heritage of British Columbia" and was appointed to the B.C. Heritage Trust board of directors in 1998 and again in 2000.

Cathryn Wellner is a storyteller, speaker and seminar leader who has toured widely in the U.S., Canada, Ireland, France and Germany. Her performances blend music and the spoken word. They have been described as "memorable" (*Wenatchee World*), "the hit of the day" (Sisters of Providence Conference), "moving and inspiring" (Antioch University) and "a wonderful mix of laughter, tears, whimsy and a lot of questions to ask oneself" (Creative Dimensions).

Wright and Wellner now live at Pioneer Ranch near Williams Lake in the Cariboo, where they operate the ranch, tour as storytellers and are partners in GrassRoots Consulting, a communications and economic development group, and Winter Quarters Press.

Their Web site is: http/grassrootsgroup.com.

The Wake Up Jacob Band

Morning comes early in a gold camp, where whoever was designated to rouse the men sometimes sang out this traditional call:

> Wake up, Jacob! Daylight's breaking
> Bacon's in the pan; coffee's in the pot.
> Get up now; get it while it's hot.

The band takes its name from the call. On "Rough but honest miner" you'll hear Richard Wright, vocals, autoharp; Cathryn Wellner, vocals; Duncan Bell, narration, vocals; Willie P. Bennett, harmonica; Ken Hamm, guitar, vocals; Caridwen Irvine, fiddle; Donna Konsorado, banjo; John Law, mandolin, vocals; Michele Law, bass, vocals; Jerry Paquette, vocals; Edd Wright, narration.

Richard Wright & Cathryn Wellner

Willie P. Bennett

Ken Hamm
Donna Konsorado

Duncan Bell

John &
Michele Law

Jerry Paquette

Caridwen Irvine

Rough but honest miner CD

Production

Produced by Ken Hamm & Richard Wright

Exec. Producers Richard Wright & Cathryn Wellner

Recorded and mixed by Jerry Paquette, Raincoast Music, Nanaimo, B.C., except tracks 5, 8, 10, 15, & 22, recorded by Len Osanic at Fiasco Bros., New Westminster, B.C.

Mastering by Bud Bremner, Coastal Mastering Studios

CD Design: Cathryn Wellner

CD printing: Precision Sound

Arrangements by the artists, ©2000

Except where noted, all words and tunes are in the public domain

Special notes

Ken Hamm plays a mid-1800s Bruno guitar.

Our thanks to Story & Co. Pianos for the loan of the 1887 Bell pump organ played by Jack Velker.

The CD (78224-11362; ISBN 0-9696887-4-1) & the companion book, *Castles in the Air* (with complete lyrics, stories & notes for each song and narration, ISBN 0-9696887-5-X), may be purchased from Winter Quarters Press, Box 15 Miocene, Williams Lake, B.C., Canada V2G 2P3 (250) 296-4432, fax (250) 296-4429; cwellner@grassrootsgroup.com. Distributed by Sandhill Book Marketing Ltd., Kelowna, B.C., (250) 763-1406, fax (250) 763-4051.

Teaching notes

For lesson plans see http:grassrootsgroup.com.

Also available from Winter Quarters Press

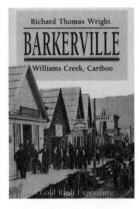

Revised Edition

BARKERVILLE

A GOLD RUSH EXPERIENCE

Over 23,000 copies in print

The historic town of Barkerville is flourishing again today as it did over 100 years ago, this time under the care of professional and amateur historians. Author Richard Wright has unearthed much of the area's history in this book, which chronicles the time, the fortunes and the follies of gold-rush Barkerville. This Canadian bestseller brings to life the men and women of the creeks who came in search of gold and left their mark on B.C. history.

Barkerville, A Gold Rush Experience is the most comprehensive source of information on this important heritage site. ISBN 0-9696887-1-7, $12.95

Richard Wright tells the epic tale of the cross-Canada treks for gold, 1858-1862, following an unexplored overland route across North America to the B.C. goldfields. This is the story of that amazing adventure. 314 pages, 50 photographs, maps, extensive footnotes & biographies. ISBN 0-9696887-3-3, $27.95

Wright and Wellner are currently working on two more books on the Cariboo goldfields. *The Great Cariboo Wagon Road* is a mile-by-mile guide to history along the Cariboo Wagon Road. The second, *Whiskey Dealers and Fallen Angels,* will look at the women who populated the gold creeks. They are also producing a series of CD's on the early music of the goldfields and British Columbia.

Order your books & CD from

Winter Quarters Press, Box 15 Miocene, Williams Lake, B.C., Canada V2G 2P3, (250) 296-4432; fax 296-4429; cwellner@grassrootsgroup.com
Distributed by Sandhill Book Marketing Ltd., (250) 763-1406, fax 763-4051.